LAMA OF THE GOBI

HOW MONGOLIA'S MYSTIC MONK
SPREAD TIBETAN BUDDHISM
IN THE WORLD'S HARSHEST DESERT

Michael Kohn

BLACKSMITH BOOKS

LAMA OF THE GOBI
How Mongolia's mystic monk spread Tibetan
Buddhism in the world's harshest desert

ISBN 978-988-17742-6-2

Published by Blacksmith Books
5th Floor, 24 Hollywood Road, Central, Hong Kong
Tel: (+852) 2877 7899
www.blacksmithbooks.com

Contents

Anyone visiting Mongolia soon hears tales of Danzan Ravjaa, the fifth reincarnate lama of the Gobi, who was officially known as the Noyon Hutagt. The role of this reincarnate lineage in the Gobi was somewhat akin to the role of the Dalai Lamas in Tibet, in that they both to some extent symbolized and were responsible for the spiritual and the social integrity of their respective realms.

The Fifth Noyon, popularly known as Ravjaa, was perhaps the greatest genius of the Noyon line, writing countless mystical poems, philosophical treatises, plays and operas. He was also the most controversial, becoming famous for his many love affairs and his unconstrained consumption of alcohol, both of which are prohibited for Buddhist monks. Mongols love him for both.

When the Soviet-backed communists took over Mongolia in the early 1920s they at first began a campaign of character assassination of him. Later, however, following the China-Soviet conflict of the 1960s, the communists began to drag him out of the closet, projecting him as anti-Chinese, anti-Old-School, and all the other "anti" labels popular with the communists of the time. His stature has only grown with the passing years.

Michael Kohn is neither an historian nor a Buddhist scholar, but rather is a wonderful investigative journalist. He brings his skills in this arena to the task, not with the aim of presenting a hard history of Ravjaa himself, but rather to reveal the manner in which the myths and legends surrounding Ravjaa play in the minds of Mongols today.

Glenn H Mullin

PREFACE

Danzan Ravjaa first came into my life in October 1999. He arrived not quite in the literal sense, but rather in the form of a newspaper article published in *The Mongol Messenger*, my employer at the time. Every so often we ran a feature story on unique personalities in Mongolian history and the article on Ravjaa was only one in a long series. Despite the obscurity of the subject matter (I had never heard of him before) I was instantly attracted to his story and the legends that surrounded him. He was described, in no uncertain terms, as a lyrical genius, master artist and gifted songwriter. His ability to perform miracles seemed only limited to the imagination of his disciples and the Gobi people who passed on his story for generations after his death. But the greatness of his artistic abilities, said the article, was matched by a legendary temper, desire for alcohol and lust for women. Almost predictably, this conflicted personality came to an almost Shakespearean end, accepting the poisoned drink of a scorned lover. Add martyr-for-love to his list of credentials.

The wild story included a surprise finish. Apparently, Danzan Ravjaa's principal monastery had recently been rebuilt and monks were once again performing services there. Better still, a museum filled with objects owned by Danzan Ravjaa had recently opened in Sainshand. Instantly intrigued by this revelation, I was determined to one day visit the museum and the nearby monastery. For a moment I imagined myself wandering about the Gobi, confronted by the mystical ghosts of a bygone era. I am a daydreamer after all, and it seemed like Danzan Ravjaa was one too.

An opportunity to visit the monastery and the museum arrived in February of 2000. With some time off from work I decided to take the train to China where I planned to visit some of the Tibetan villages in Gansu and Sichuan. About halfway between Ulaanbaatar and the Chinese border the train stopped in Sainshand. It was two in the morning and the temperature was minus 25 degrees Celsius. My thick down coat and insulated boots barely kept the cold out, but before long I found my way to the only hotel in town. The following day I paid a visit to the museum and was amazed to see the wealth of artifacts that it housed. Theater costumes, Buddhist art and Ravjaa's personal effects were but a few of the items on display. As the only visitor to the museum, the curator Altangerel provided a personalized tour. He went into great detail about the life and legend of Danzan Ravjaa and our conversation carried straight into lunch. Enthralled by the stories, I finally asked Altangerel where he had acquired so much knowledge about this obscure historical figure. And here is where the story got better – Altangerel explained that he was the direct descendant of Danzan Ravjaa's personal attendant. The life and legend of the great monk had been passed down through the generations until it had reached Altangerel.

Not only had stories been passed, but also the right to maintain all of his worldly possessions. Altangerel was the sixth-generation curator of these precious goods. The story was incredible, made more so by the fact that 70 years of communism had cut most Mongolians off from the distant past. Somehow, Altangerel had managed to bridge the gap of that dark era in Mongolia's history.

Over the coming days I paid a visit to the monastery (known as Khamaryn Khiid), met the monks that maintained it and clambered through a cave that supposedly cleansed me of my sins. I tasted water from a spring with healing powers, stumbled upon a dinosaur bone and mounted an unruly camel. Back in Sainshand, Altangerel showed me some of his most prized possessions, many of them too valuable to be on display in a museum that had no security system.

While sifting through all this history was a fascinating experience, much of it was lost on me as there was precious little written about Danzan Ravjaa in the English language. Any research done in Mongolian seemed either too fanciful or too academic. I struggled to make sense of all that lay before me. I guessed that other foreign visitors to the museum would be equally baffled and decided to help out by creating an information pamphlet in English. That initial pamphlet seemed to grow by the day as I kept stumbling over new sources of information. At some point my short essay had morphed into the book you are holding.

A good deal of the research conducted for this book was made during subsequent visits to Sainshand and Khamaryn Khiid. More research was conducted in Ulaanbaatar, where I interviewed experts, scholars and academics familiar with the life of Danzan Ravjaa. I also spent considerable time in the stacks of the Ulaanbaatar Public Library, digging through a vast array of books related to both Ravjaa and his contemporaries. Much of the credit for the compilation of Danzan Ravjaa's life story goes to the Mongolian researchers Ts. Damdinsuren, D. Tsagaan and the German researcher Walther Heissig.

So far as the orthography is concerned, I have tried to use the most common and simple transliteration for Mongolian words and names. Place names have changed over the years, and I have chosen to include the ones used when the reference was compiled: for example, I call Ulaanbaatar "Huree" when describing the city before the 1920s. In many cases I simply used what sounded most appropriate. Getting Danzan Ravjaa's poetry into a form of English both readable and accurate was somewhat problematic because of the three-stage translation: it was originally written in Tibetan, converted to old Mongolian, then to Cyrillic (new Mongolian) and finally translated to English. I applaud the efforts of my translators for doing the most accurate job possible.

The majority of quotations used are taken from books of the period written by travelers including the Abbé Huc, Aleksei Pozdneyev and Col N. Przewalski, and are sourced accordingly. However, the quotes attributed to Danzan Ravjaa (taken from Mongolian history books, or from oral storytelling), should be considered as mere guesses as to what he might have said.

I must state that much of what has been recorded about Danzan Ravjaa is fiction or contradictory. There were no real journalistic accounts or records of what he was like and scant information about the activities of his monasteries. Much of the research herein was pieced together from the most reliable and reasonable sources. Much of it is simply guesswork. I note where stories and historical evidence conflict and I include discrepancies in the text or endnotes.

Piecing together the story of Danzan Ravjaa and writing this book was a labor of love that continued over several years. After sitting for a very long time as a stack of white papers that was passed from hand to hand, it eventually reached renowned Tibetologist Glenn Mullin. A connoisseur of all things esoteric, Glenn took an interest in the manuscript and helped to get it published for the first time in 2006. Half the books were donated to Altangerel in Sainshand so that he might raise money for a much-needed security system for the museum.

I wrote this book largely because it was fun and fresh. In a world where it seems everything is "been-there-done-that," I managed to find a piece of history almost unknown to Westerners. It simply seemed like a story too interesting to ignore. In the future I hope that more extensive information in English will be made available on Ravjaa's complex philosophy, his poetry, his operas, his artwork and the world in which he lived. And to anyone who reads this book, I hope that you will one day have the chance to visit Khamaryn Khiid and be touched by its soul.

Michael Kohn
San Francisco, March 2010

MONGOLIA

Tuva

RUSSIA

Buryatia

Manchuria

Khövsgöl

Amarbayasgalant

Ulaanbaatar
(Khuree)

Karakorum
(Erdene Zuu)

Sainshand
(Khamaryn Khiid)

Gobi Desert

Doloon Nuur

Beijing (Peking)

CHINA

Amdo
(Tibet)

INTRODUCTION

The year is 1937; the place is Dornogobi Province, Mongolia. The following is a dramatized account based on real events.

The stars over Khamaryn Monastery twinkle like diamonds strewn across the inky heavens. The earth below is silent and hot, still radiating heat hours after the setting of the Gobi sun. Silhouettes of temple rooftops rise and dip across the night skyline. This would be an otherwise peaceful scene for Lama Tuduv as he sits awake that night. But the young Buddhist monk has weighty subjects on his mind. His monastery is in danger; his life is in danger, as are the lives of all the other monks at Khamaryn Khiid.

It's 1937 and Communist oppression is building not only at Khamaryn Khiid but all across Mongolia. Warnings have already been sent to the monastery that it will be shut down. Soldiers have harassed the monks, accusing them of 'counter-revolutionary activities'. Lama Tuduv and his fellow monks can see the writing on the wall; their monastery will be destroyed and they must save what they can before it's too late. Their Buddha Danzan Ravjaa had predicted all of this.

Since a young age Lama Tuduv had been sworn to the defense of Danzan Ravjaa and he is determined to protect the monastery's sacred relics at all costs. Fortunately, he is not alone. All the monks at Khamaryn Khiid are willing to lay down their lives to protect the monastery.

Carefully, cautiously, Tuduv and several assistant lamas begin the arduous task of removing the sacred objects from the White Temple, preparing to bury them in the desert. Moving and burying dozens of crates seems like an impossible goal to Tuduv but there are few alternative options. Wiping sweat from his brow, Tuduv banishes such thoughts with a grunt and continues his work.

By the light of a small oil lamp the red-cloaked monks can make out the sacred relics of the temple. Piles of Buddhist manuscripts and sutras, masks and costumes used in sacred rituals, theater props used in plays, artwork delicately sculpted and painted by master craftsmen, and valuable objects brought from foreign lands. Despite its name, the White Temple is not a place of worship; rather it's a museum of sorts, founded by Ravjaa to show off his finest possessions. The center of the building contains its most unique object, the mummified remains of Danzan Ravjaa, the master poet, artist, pedagogue and saint who had founded Khamaryn Khiid some 120 years earlier.

It's no accident that most of this priceless treasure is already packed into wooden crates. The categorizing and recording of items had already been prepared for just such an emergency evacuation. With the utmost care and silence, Tuduv opens one of the crates and inspects it, studying the items inside. The significance of each piece had been made known to him by his father Ongoi, who had instructed Tuduv from birth on the history of Danzan Ravjaa and Khamaryn Khiid. Tuduv's ancestors, dating back four generations to his great-great-grandfather Balchinchoijoo, had always assumed responsibility for the relics left behind by Danzan Ravjaa. The family legacy weighs heavily on Lama Tuduv's shoulders as he ponders the days ahead. The soldiers will soon make their move to destroy the monastery and the monks will be unable to defend it. There is no time to lose.

Stealthily, the monks carry the crates out of the temple and begin their trek into the desert. The stars have shifted considerably by the time Tuduv and the others reach a steep ravine cut into the desert floor. Sunk out of sight from the enormous plains, the ravine is the most logical place around Khamaryn Khiid to hide the treasure-filled crates. With the full moon rising overhead they dig a hole and together chant a mantra asking forgiveness for digging in the sacred earth. When it's deep enough, the monks place the box in the hole, covering it with rocks and soil.

Resting for a moment in the light of the moon, Tuduv breathes deeply and nods off to sleep. Dreams rush to him and in his troubled mind he sees the young soldiers setting temples alight; the whitewashed walls charred black as the elegant concave roof collapses. The soldiers then turn their guns on the rows of red-robed monks. Plumes of smoke rise in the air as they fall face-first into a mass grave. Tuduv winces in the dark as blood is shed and the precious legacy of Danzan Ravjaa – Mongolia's greatest poet and lyricist – is wiped out in a matter of minutes.

Startled awake by the nightmare, Tuduv rises to his feet and realizes that he is still safe, for the moment anyway. He chants softly to himself, praying that his visions will end, yet he knows the destruction is inevitable. Lama Tuduv and the monks return to Khamaryn Khiid in silence, arriving just before the dawn.

Each night thereafter, the monks repeat the process of filling up crates and hauling them into the desert. Laymen nomads living around the monastery are warned of the pending disaster and respond by hiding their personal property deep in the desert. Families are digging holes in the earth and burying Buddhas all across the Gobi.

For several weeks the monks and laymen are able to secretly hide their sacred objects but in the middle of the summer the situation changes for the worse. Trucks carrying soldiers arrive with orders to destroy the monastery. When the monks protest they are arrested and taken away.

Lama Tuduv is not among the arrested monks. He manages to escape the chaos and the other monks have sworn to keep his identity a secret.

Lama Tuduv turns his worried heart away from the abandoned monastery and travels deep into the Gobi. He heads south and eventually reaches a *ger* (yurt) owned by his sister. Here he will stay to wait out the storm of death and destruction.

Skip ahead to 1991...

A cloud of dust billows up from the yellow earth as three men dig their heels into shovels and turn over dirt. One looks up for a moment to survey the land. A great monastery once stood not far from where the men dig. Khamaryn Khiid was a monastery of whitewashed walls and ornately painted wooden eaves, home to young students and learned scholars, a monastery with cavernous temples from which the sounds of conch shell trumpets once blew. Now there is nothing but dry barren desert and stray camels. Nothing remains of its glorious past.

Three feet below the surface, one of the men strikes something hard with his shovel. Sand and rocks are brushed away and a wooden box is revealed. The men run their fingers over the warped wood, perhaps to absorb some of its secrets. Altangerel had been correct; with no map he had found one of the boxes buried by his grandfather Tuduv, who had died only a few months earlier. The men congratulate each other and then lift the heavy crate out of the ground and into an olive-green Russian jeep. Rolling over the low hills and gravelly earth they return home in silence.

Altangerel, trained as the latest in a long line of Danzan Ravjaa curators, opens the crate carefully as a crowd of onlookers loom overhead. Daylight floods into the box for the first time in many years. He reaches a large hand inside and extracts the porcelain statue of a Chinese princess. Her intricate design and colorful detail are a wonder for these people of the Gobi. Having lived under the veil of communism for so many years, this generation knows little of their past. But this box is proof that something amazing had occurred here many years ago.

Altangerel too is fascinated, although he has seen these objects before. Years earlier, his grandfather Lama Tuduv had dug up this very box and showed him its contents. Tuduv had described each item in detail so that when the time was right, Altangerel would be able to properly recount the legacy of Danzan Ravjaa. That time, it seems, has finally arrived.

Based on the lifelong lessons given by his grandfather, Altangerel returns to the desert and the secret places where the boxes had been buried. Altangerel digs up nearly half of the sixty-four crates. The boxes are cared for and treated with wonder, as though an ancient past had been reincarnated into a living, breathing element. Indeed, it has. The legend of Danzan Ravjaa, once just a series of myths passed around between lonely nomads of the Gobi Desert, has at last been revealed as truth.

The story of these boxes, where they came from and why, will be told in this book.

Shambala, a sacred spot near Danzan Ravjaa's monastery

The Mysterious Monk

Is there wine? Then drink!
Is there a song? Then sing!
Are there thoughts? Then talk!
Is there brandy? Then drink!
Danzan Ravjaa

The Gobi Desert has long been one of the most inhospitable places on Earth. Dreaded by early Western explorers, the Gobi was infamous for being able to kill a man in any number of ways. Dust storms blew away camps; bandits were a constant threat; the summer heat sizzled the skin; the winter cold froze a person to the bone. Abbé Huc, a French missionary who traveled through Inner Mongolia in 1842, wrote in his book *Travels in Tartary, Thibet and China:*

> "In Tartary, there are no towns, no edifices, no arts,
> no industry, no cultivation, no forests; everywhere it
> is prairie, sometimes interrupted by immense lakes, by
> majestic rivers, by rugged and imposing mountains;

sometimes spreading out into vast limitless plains. There in these verdant solitudes, the bounds of which seem lost in the remote horizon, you might imagine yourself gently rocking on the calm waves of some broad ocean."[1]

This does not seem the sort of place one would expect to find a drama theater or a genius. One would certainly not expect to find here a Renaissance figure capable of producing sophisticated artwork and lyrically brilliant poetry. And it seems unlikely that one might find – in 19th-century China – a respected education center in a remote corner of the Manchu Empire. It is surprising then, that such a person and such a place did exist. The genius referred to is Danzan Ravjaa, the fifth Dogshin Noyon Hutagt, or Incarnate Lama, of the Gobi Desert – one of the most complex and misunderstood personalities in the history of Mongolia. He has been called a drunken womanizer, a madman, an uncompromising tyrant, and a heretic. But he has also been called a genius, a living Buddha, a social critic, a man of compassion and a champion of human rights. In some ways, from different perspectives, he may have been all of these.

If Danzan Ravjaa were alive today his critics would probably label him a practitioner of "Gonzo Buddhism." One hundred and fifty years ago he went by similar-sounding monikers. His official Buddhist title was "Ikh Gobi Dogshin Noyon Hutagt," the "Fierce Lord, Saint of the Great Gobi."

Much of his life was spent as a wandering cleric, visiting monasteries across Inner and Outer Mongolia, and training students in the principles and practices of Vajrayana Buddhism. Yet Ravjaa's interests were by no means limited to Buddhism;

he wrote poetry, staged dramatic theater, choreographed music, practiced herbal medicine and created works of art in a variety of mediums.

When not traveling, Danzan Ravjaa spent much of his time in monastic institutes and meditation hermitages in Alasha (Alxa), Doloon Nuur (Doloo) and Chahar, as well as his own specially built facilities in two different regions of Outer Mongolia. His main monastery complex was Khamaryn Khiid, in the eastern Gobi Desert (modern Dornogobi). The religious services he hosted were usually accompanied by games, festivities and feasting. His reputation was so widespread that students of Buddhism from Japan, China, Tibet and Korea spent time studying at his monastery. Dignitaries and princes of these countries also paid him tribute with gifts and honorific titles.

Among his talents, Ravjaa is best known for his powerfully emotive poetry and plays. Until very recently, his writings had been lost, forgotten by modern Mongols. It is only since the late 1990s that his works (dozens of songs and more than 300 poems) have been rediscovered and Danzan Ravjaa is now considered, quite simply, Mongolia's greatest writer and playwright. His operatic-drama *Life Story of the Moon Cuckoo* (*Saran Khökhöö Namtar*) was the first modern theater production in Mongolia, and surely a unique event in the Gobi Desert. To perform his masterpiece, he built Mongolia's first playhouse, a colossal three-story complex constructed at Khamaryn Khiid.

The opera was so popular that he took it on the road. Like a 12th-century European troubadour, Ravjaa traveled between monasteries with his performers, packing his costumes into chests and placing them on the backs of sturdy two-humped camels. *Saran Khökhöö*, performed regularly until the 1920s, is still one of the best-known plays in Mongolia, studied by academics and artists alike.

Ravjaa, whose life, interests and achievements very much reflect those ascribed to the unconventional Sixth Dalai Lama, was also a recognized medicine man and tantric practitioner. Utilizing a combination of natural herbs and prayers to heal the sick, Ravjaa treated countless Mongols (mainly common nomads) during his travels. He was also trusted to care for nobles and even Mongolia's spiritual leader, the Bogd Gegeen of Huree.

Legend speaks of his predilection to cleanliness. He had his own bathing *ger*, equipped with a large round tub where he washed himself and invited friends to scrub off the desert dust. Afterwards, guests were served his finest *arkhi* (distilled alcohol, made from cow or horse milk) and dabbed with perfumes imported from China. This must have been a remarkable experience for those dust-caked Gobi dwellers, for whom bathing was generally a foreign concept.

Ravjaa's bathing ger, not to mention his temples and libraries, were by no means kept exclusive. People of all social standing, rank and gender were invited to join him in his activities and events. He mixed with the locals: ate, drank, prayed and bathed with them. Despite his fine silk clothing and crimson monk's robes, he never shied away from the Gobi nomads and the most common or commoners. Such a man was certainly rare in 19th-century Mongolia.

Why then did this wealthy, powerful and talented man reach out to the poorest members of society?

The answer perhaps lies in his childhood. Ravjaa was a man of the Gobi, born onto its sands and under its blistering sun. There is something about the raw power of this massive and forbidding desert that makes men equal, a trait Ravjaa carried with him to the grave. Having lived his youth as a poor beggar, he was emotionally close not merely to his disciples but also ordinary Gobi dwellers. Although elevated to a more prominent status at a young age, Danzan Ravjaa still carried with him the sorrow and misery that he experienced during the first six years of his life. These hardships are often reflected in his poetry and plays.

Ravjaa's adulthood was somehow an extension of this difficult and unstructured childhood. Rules and regulations, particularly when they applied to conservative Buddhism, were generally flaunted. Celibacy and abstention from alcohol, for example, were by no means a part of his life.

His religious beliefs, however, seemed consistent with traditional Mongolian teachings. He was not (contrary to popular belief) merely a follower of the Red Tradition (Nyingma, Red Hat), but rather combined both the Red and Yellow (Gelugpa) faiths. This was common practice for Buddhism in Mongolia, which from the time of the great Zanabazar (1634-1723) was built on the lineages of the Fifth Dalai Lama and the First Panchen Lama, both of whom combined the Gelugpa and Nyingma traditions in their personal lives.

Once when asked whether or not he was Nyingma or Gelugpa, Ravjaa replied "Buddha's right arm is the Red School and his left is the Yellow School. Would you like me to tear Buddha in half?" Danzan Ravjaa used this metaphor because Padmasambhava, the founder of the Nyingma tradition, is considered an incarnation of Avalokiteshvara, the Buddha of compassion, a quality associated with the right side of the body; whereas Tsongkhapa, the founder of the Gelugpa tradition, is seen as an incarnation of Manjushri, wisdom, a quality associated with the left part of the body.

Ravjaa's faith in the Gelugpa is further described in the following verse:

> Between vessel and essence,
> The essence is the great one.
> Among the four great continents,
> Jambudvipa is the great one.
> Of all forms of life, a fully qualified
> Precious human rebirth is the great one.
> Of all lineages from Buddha Shakyamuni,
> The Yellow School Lineage is the great one.
> And of the Jewels of Refuge,
> Refuge in the lama is supreme[2]

Despite his self-proclaimed allegiance to the Yellow tradition, Ravjaa did not always enjoy warm relations with all the mainstream Gelugpa leaders, especially those in Huree, because of conflicting social and political beliefs. He was by all accounts a man not afraid to question authority or criticize people of low ethical standards.

His lifestyle was another matter of contention. Sex and alcohol were his favored preoccupations and he often made note of this in many of his poems, which ended with lines such as: "the drunken one wrote this."

His exploits earned him nicknames from capital city residents, who called him 'the crazy one' and 'the wild drunk of the Gobi'. His hot-headed personality only added to this reputation. Legend tells of his launching into fits of uncontrollable fury at the most banal of incidents. Danzan Ravjaa knew himself all too well when he wrote:

My strong and true mind
Is out of kilter with the world
My ill-tempered nature
Is out of kilter with local customs[3]

This temperamental personality resulted in a somewhat lonely existence. Unable to deal with others in these times of private madness, Ravjaa occasionally retreated to desert caves for days on end. He even owned a ger with no door; his disciples knew not to disturb him once he had slipped under the wall. This must have been extremely unusual amongst a people known for their great hospitality, social customs and family ties.

Yet Ravjaa was unlike other Mongols. Mentally and spiritual higher than his peers, a gap was always in evidence. These unique circumstances earned him the moniker *Dogshin*, which directly translates as "terrible," or possibly in Danzan Ravjaa's case, "wrathful," which not only displays a sense of power, but also respect.[4]

Danzan Ravjaa's complex personality became a seed of myths and legends. Typical of a folk hero, the stories about Ravjaa's deeds have been highly exaggerated or simply created. Indeed, much of his entire life seems like a fairy tale, contrived by creative nomads with plenty of time on their hands. Aleksei Pozdneyev, who traveled in Mongolia in the late 19th century, made careful note of this after visiting a number of Mongol *huvilgans* (reincarnate lamas). Pozdneyev wrote,

> "There is almost no possibility of getting a true notion of the life of huvilgan from the stories of Mongols themselves. Filled with reverence for their holy persons, they besprinkle

their entire life with unprecedented miracles, from the moment of conception until death itself. Just try and ask a Mongol about the life of some gegeen, and you will hear without fail that his parents were a model of purity and devotion, that the huvilgan's conception happened in a certain way, that his stay in his mother's womb was accompanied by numerous dreams meaningful to her; that the birth itself did not pass without some miracle, that the child from his first days, weeks or months displayed unusual abilities; his first words were the words of some prayer, and so on and so on."[5]

As we will see later, many of these myths surrounding Ravjaa are connected with his travels, his miraculous deeds and his affairs with women. Some of the stories are long, drawn-out, biblical-type adventures. Others are little factoids that Gobi people like to bring up in conversation. I was once told, for example, why no recognizable photograph of Ravjaa exists. Apparently, various foreign travelers tried to snap his picture, but the image of him always came out as a featureless dark figure, as if he were a ghost, or had the power to sabotage a camera using mental telepathy.[6]

There are hundreds of other tall tales related to Ravjaa. Although most were collected after the 1960s, more than 100 years after Ravjaa's death, the stories can be beneficial to the historian if compared with what few factual accounts have been revealed about his life. Not only do similar patterns occur, but they also lend insight into 19th-century Mongol life and provide necessary clues as to how common people viewed this monk. The wild and erratic stories earned Ravjaa a special place in Mongolian history as a social commentator, an independent thinker, and as a rebel.

His folk hero status is strongest in his native Dornogobi Aimag, home to his famed Khamaryn monastery. Today, the playhouse in the provincial capital Sainshand is called 'Saran Khökhöö Theater' and the curtains inside are embellished with two large embroidered scorpions – the creature Ravjaa respected most and used on his own personal seal. There is a museum dedicated to Ravjaa and his possessions. It has become a sort of pilgrimage site for scholars of Mongol literature.

More recently, Ravjaa has become an important figure of study for researchers, writers and artists. He is, however, virtually unknown outside the Mongol world. My hope is that this book will reveal his life to an ever-greater audience.

* * *

Ravjaa was the fifth incarnation of the Gobi Noyon Hutagts. Two more would eventually follow for a total of seven. These 'Gobi Saints' are all the product of another line of incarnates that originated in Tibet and India. Each incarnate is an emanation of a single Buddhist tantric deity called Yansang Yidam, who is associated with wizardry, power, genius and healing. This mandala deity is also known as Damdin, which is Hayagriva in Sanskrit.

Traditional biographical literature on the Noyon incarnates documents a large number of lives prior to the appearance of the first Noyon in Mongolia. The Danzan Ravjaa Museum in Sainshand has paintings of approximately 30 of them, some of whom are believed to have lived more than 1000 years ago. A few of these pre-incarnations are well-known historical figures, including the fourth Karmapa Lama, who is listed as the 22nd incarnation. Another well-known part of this line was Kukuripa, one of the 84 mahasiddhas of India. It is most likely that the line of incarnates was assembled following the death of the First Noyon Hutagt.

The richness of this line of incarnations is an indication of how deeply rooted Danzan Ravjaa must have considered his place in the Buddhist realm. On display at the Danzan Ravjaa Museum is a set of paintings which shows off many of these past incarnations. Each framed painting shows one incarnation in meditation or yogic pose. Clearly the artist used several figures in Buddhist lore as models. The painting of the first incarnation, for example, is modeled after Amithaba. The sixth incarnation, Zanaadaraa, bears a striking resemblance to Milarepa.

Each incarnation is painted in a pose that signifies special abilities gained as a by-product of meditational thought. The third incarnation, for example, is shown as a bookkeeper and author of sutras (books appear slung over his shoulder). The 11th is shown in front of a cave, representing the 40 years he spent in isolation. The 20th could travel long distances in an instant. For a complete listing of these incarnations, see the appendix of this book.

The Mongolia link picks up steam with Sanjaibalsan, the 32nd incarnate. This holy man had a Mongolian student under his tutelage and one day the eager disciple asked his teacher to be reborn in Mongolia in his next life. As the student was his favorite, Sanjaibalsan agreed to the proposal. Thus, after the Tibetan master died, his students sought the next incarnation in Mongolia.

And if locating one huvilgan would promote Buddhism in Mongolia, finding three would be even more auspicious. According to instructions given to students of Sanjaibalsan, three children were found in Outer Mongolia, each embodying an aspect of the previous incarnation. One child, found in modern day Bulgan Aimag, was named Khangalchingellin Adoochin Hutagt, or "The Wild Cowboy Saint". A second, found in modern-day Övörkhangai

Aimag, was called Nomj Mergen, "Wise and Educated". The last was found in modern day Dornogobi: he was called Dogshin Sogtuu Hutagt, "Fierce and Drunk Saint", but is better known by his Tibetan name – Agvangonchig.

It was said that later in life, the cowboy saint loved horses, the wise saint was fond of reading holy texts and the drunken saint had the power to change vodka into medicine. It was this last incarnation that was recognized as the First Gobi Noyon Hutagt (1621-1703).

* * *

Agvangonchig was born into an aristocratic family that claimed direct descent from Batmönkh Dayan Khaan, the boy-king who ruled Mongolia from 1470-1504. With royal blood in his veins young Agvangonchig could later claim both spiritual and temporal powers. His father was Sonam Daichinkhun Taij, a mid-level aristocrat of Mandlai sum in present day Ömnögobi Aimag. Following recognition, the young Hutagt was sent to Lhasa for ordination and training; he stayed there for over 30 years. Agvangonchig returned to his homeland as a middle-aged man and began the construction of a new temple. His Amgalan Temple[7], completed in 1666, was the first ever built in Gobi Mergen Van Khoshuu. As the years passed more temples were built around it and the complex came to be known as Tsorai Monastery, which doubled as both a holy place and as the home of the Gobi Mergen Van. [8]

Before a huvilgan dies, he will usually leave instructions about where to find his next incarnation. After three or four years his disciples begin to search for the young incarnate, a process that can take months or even years. This is the process that occurred following the death of the First Noyon Hutagt. The young child was eventually located in Tulagt, about six miles south of present-day Sainshand. Although his father was an ordinary livestock breeder, the child Jamyn Dambi Jantsen exhibited extraordinary talents that marked him as an incarnated saint. The Second Hutagt (1704-1739) is believed to have built the ill-fated Choilong Monastery at Tulagt. This monastery, located at the foot of Bayan Zurkh Uul (Rich Heart Mountain), was reduced to cinders soon after its construction, when an oil lamp tipped over and torched the buildings.[9] The temples were rebuilt twice, each time leveled by fierce sand storms. By the end of the 18th century the monastery was completely abandoned.

Jamyn Dambi Jantsen died at the young age of 35 and his body was interred at Agvangonchig's Amgalan temple. Years later, in 1833, Danzan Ravjaa moved his remains to a small sanctuary near the ruins of Choilong Monastery.

More is known about the Third Noyon Hutagt, Jamyn Danzan (approximate life dates: 1740-1765), although the Russian and the Mongolian accounts utterly contradict one another.

According to the Russian writer Pozdneyev, the Third Hutagt was little more than a highwayman who had no time for Buddhism because he was too busy looking for caravans to rob. He enjoyed hunting most of all but when there were no animals to kill the young lama and his friends bided their time ambushing passing traders. For this, Pozdneyev states, he became known to all and sundry as "Dogshin", or "The Terrible." So notorious was his gang of desert pirates that road traffic near Choilong Monastery stopped, as traders feared crossing it. His most brazen attack came in 1765 when the hutagt stole a cache of silver that was being delivered from the Manchu court in Peking to Tsetsen Khaan Aimag.

The Hutagt evaded punishment from the Tusheet Khaan nobility by paying them tribute but the Manchu authorities were not so easily bribed. For months he hid out in the desert, sleeping in caves, traveling by night and surviving with the aid of sympathetic local families. Manchu loyalists eventually captured the hutagt, put him in chains and brought him to Peking. China's Ministry for Tibetan and Mongolian Affairs examined the case, found the Hutagt guilty (murder and theft the likely charges) and sentenced him to death. He was just 25 years old.

As they had done with previous lines of incarnate lamas who had stirred up trouble, the Manchus prohibited the search for a new incarnate Noyon Hutagt.[10]

This account is completely unknown to Mongolians who paint a starkly different picture of the Third Hutagt, presenting him as a well-respected and praiseworthy monk, and as a highly talented writer, builder and meditation teacher. They know him best for his construction of a temple at Tengeriin Takhiilgat Uul (Sacrifice to Heaven Mountain) in Dornogobi Province. According to popular legend, when the Third Noyon Hutagt meditated on this mountain the deity Khaand appeared riding atop a dragon and bestowed special meditative powers upon him.

Although Mongolian versions of Jamyn Danzan's life story are full of praise, the stories of his father are less flattering. He was a nobleman called Tseden Mergen Zasag who had borrowed money from a Tangut trader, had used it for public works projects, but had failed to repay the loan.

There is a legend about what happened next. According to the story, the Tangut man died soon after, but even in the afterlife he never forgot about losing his money to Tseden Mergen Zasag, and complained to Erlig (the King of the Underworld). Shortly thereafter, Tseden Mergen himself died and was brought before Erlig, where he found the Tangut man waiting with crossed arms and pursed lips. An argument erupted over the money and Tseden denied that he was in debt to the Tangut. Seeking to resolve the dispute in a just manner, Erlig called Tseden's son, the Third Noyon Hutagt, to act as a witness. His spirit was brought to the underworld from his place of meditation in the Gobi and Erlig questioned him over the incident.

Honest as he was, Jamyn Danzan confirmed that his father had not returned the money. This response pleased Erlig, and the Tseden Mergen Zasag was punished. For his honesty, the spirit of Jamyn Danzan was allowed to return to Earth, but when the spirit came upon his body he found that it had already been pickled and mummified by the lamas of Choilong Khiid! Because his spirit had been absent for such a long period of time, the monks assumed he had died. Unable to re-enter his dead body, his spirit entered the nearby Bayan Zurkh Uul, where it still lives today.

Another account states that the mummified body of Jamyn Danzan was originally interred at Choilong Monastery. However, after the temple was destroyed by fire the remains were scattered on Bayan Zurkh Uul.

The mountain has since become an important place of pilgrimage. It is here that one can make requests to the spirit of the Third Noyon Hutagt. Oddly, in the mid-1800s, a new law instituted by Manchu authorities decreed that all requests made on Bayan Zurkh Uul had to be announced out loud. A clerk was on hand to record the requests, to ensure that no negative statements were being said about the Emperor or the Manchu Empire.[11] Censorship in 19th-century China, it seems, stretched literally to the most distant mountaintops.

In 1990, a resident of Sainshand, a certain Gombo, constructed a small temple on Bayan Zurkh Uul and called it Sharliin süm (Corpse Temple). Visitors still come here to make requests. These no longer have to be made out loud.

If one believes Pozdneyev's account, it should be noted that the followers of Jamyn Danzan did not heed the warning of the Manchu Emperor. The Gobi dwellers had it in mind that a Fourth incarnation would indeed be located and the legacy would not end. Disciples of the Third Hutagt secretly continued their search for the next incarnation. They eventually found him in Selenge Aimag. The year was 1769.

Young Jamyn Oidov Jampts grew up to become a distinguished and famed lama. But like his predecessor, he also came to an early end, an incident to be discussed later.

Danzan Ravjaa was the incarnation to follow Jamyn Oidov Jampts, after which two more Noyon Hutagts were found. The last one, the seventh, died in 1931.

Stupa at the Mountain of the Third Hutagt

2

THE TORCH IS PASSED

If we are to believe the Russian accounts of the Third Noyon Hutagt, which ascribe his infamy for wild horseman deeds, then the fourth was just as well known for his pious acts. Jamyn Oidov Jampts was born in 1765 and dedicated his life to promoting Buddhism in Mongolia. He was widely known as a healer and dispensed medicines as he wandered between monasteries. Most of all, he was known for his excellent singing voice. Many of his disciples made pilgrimages to Zuun Khashant Monastery, which he established in modern-day Zuunbayan sum.

This greatness, however, would be overshadowed by one reckless and tragic moment that sealed his fate.

The facts of the story have been muddled over time but according to legend, in the year 1800, the famed Erdene Zuu Monastery was struck by a plague of field mice. Locals referred to these tiny, destructive rodents as *shulmuss*, or "female devils." The lamas at Erdene Zuu prayed night and day to rid their temples of these pests, which were chewing away at the wood foundations, causing serious structural damage. Yet none of their prayers seemed to have any effect on the mice, whose numbers were multiplying rapidly.

To halt the disaster, the monks felt they needed a higher authority to appease what they believed was an angry deity. Messages were dispatched to other monasteries requesting the help of skilled lamas. Jamyn Oidov Jampts, never one to turn down a challenge, responded to Erdene Zuu's plea for help.

The Hutagt mounted his horse and began the long journey to Erdene Zuu. Two hundred years ago, relay stations and gers allowed travelers a place to stop and rest during their journey. The stations were primarily set up to serve mail carriers in need of fresh horses but common travelers were also permitted to use them. For Jamyn Oidov Jampts, the relay stations were also places to sample the local *airag*, or koumiss, fermented horse milk.

A feast was held in Jamyn Oidov Jampts' honor upon his arrival at Erdene Zuu and more alcohol – brandy and airag – was consumed. The extermination of the mice began with a special ceremony that included the reading of sutras followed by the lighting of an herbal potion called *zai*, which fumigated the temple halls. This technique seemed to work as the mice soon disappeared from sight.

Jamyn Oidov Jampts enjoyed the praise of his peers following the successful round of prayers and more alcohol was drunk in celebration. He led them in song and rowdy banter. Then to amuse himself in his drunkenness, Jamyn wandered around Erdene Zuu, admiring the fine horses of this grassland area.

During his walk, so the story says, Jamyn Oidov Jampts was stopped by a Mongolian *taij*, a nobleman, who had recently married the daughter of an important Manchurian court official. He had been given the daughter as a reward for his loyalty to the emperor.

"Hutagt! You know nothing of Mongolian horses. You are from the Gobi. Why don't you stick with assessing camels?" sneered the taij.

"I am a Mongolian," replied Jamyn Oidov Jampts, insinuating that the taij was merely a traitor for marrying into a Manchu family. "So I know about both horses and camels." The taij protested and soon the quarrel erupted into a fistfight. At some point during this brawl between the lama and the nobleman, with a crowd of onlookers watching, the hutagt drew a dagger from his belt and plunged it into the prince. The mortal blow had the taij on the ground in an instant, dying in a pool of blood.

There are actually several versions of this story. Z. Altangerel, the curator of the Danzan Ravjaa Museum, told this version to me. Another common version states that the Fourth Hutagt stabbed one of his own disciples as punishment for eating mice. The young lama died of his wounds and the Hutagt was arrested.

While there might be debate over the details of the incident, there was no doubting the severity of the crime. When news of the incident reached the authorities, soldiers were dispatched to arrest the 31-year-old Hutagt and bring him to Peking. The monk was under no false illusions about the fate that lay before him, knowing full well the penalties for murder.

Escorted by Chinese Imperial guardsmen, Jamyn Oidov Jampts crossed Inner Mongolia with his personal attendant Jigmid Gonchig and headed straight for Peking. Meanwhile, fearing retribution, the disciples of Jamyn Oidov Jampts collected his possessions from Zuun Khashant and sent them to the Bogd Gegeen in Huree where they would remain safe.

En route to Peking, the monk composed a song of regret named after a horse called Naran Zul Khul. The lyrics describe in verse the monk's desire to return to the youthful innocence of a foal and spread virtuous acts. He writes that in his youth he will read books and pray, in his youth he will sweep away sin and shoot down his enemies. It is a song of hope and a plea for peace.

Sunny Bright Brown
When she was a foal
On six important books
I wish to pray

Healthy and beautiful Brown
She was quiet and young
White lotus book
I should have prayed

Brown's mouth is black
She was a kind foal
Ten black sins
Sweep away, sweep straight away

Brown's mouth is white
She was a kind foal
Ten white virtuous acts
Spread, spread them straight out

The big spreading bow
Pointing the sharp arrow
Spots of the animal like a toxic enemy
I will hold your body and hunt you from horseback

Trees looking like a crowd
When branches and leaves are fully grown

What is so interesting
They are the same

This song's name is
Sunny Bright Brown
This song was composed by
The precious Prince Saint

In the great country
Be safe and quiet
In the Khan's country
Let's meet together and enjoy all good things[12]

Jamyn Oidov Jampts told his attendant Jigmid Gonchig that he would not return to Mongolia. When they arrived in Peking Jigmid Gonchig was instructed by his lord to buy a fresh horse from the market. When Jamyn Oidov Jampts saw the horse he called it Boriv Kheer ("Chestnut") and nicknamed his friend 'Jintu' ("Pillow"), in honor of the 'comfort' he had given him. The Hutagt then leaned towards the horse and whispered his life story into its ear, and explained to 'Jintu' that they would have some connection in his next life through this horse.

Following Jintu's departure, Jamyn Oidov Jampts asked to see one of the Emperor's *juntung* (advisors). The juntung came to the dark prison cell holding the monk and asked why he had been summoned. Peering into the gloom, Jamyn Oidov Jampts took the juntung's hand and pressed into it a silver knife and fire starter. "Take them with you on your next journey to Mongolia," the monk said. "They will help you identify the next incarnation. Do not harm the boy. The lineage must continue and you will be rewarded." The juntung agreed and left the monk in silence.

The Fourth Noyon Hutagt was executed the following day and a proclamation was made, just as had been done following the death of the Third, decreeing that no more Gobi Noyon Hutagts would be permitted.

Manchurian policy makers intended to reduce the number of huvilgans in Outer Mongolia and they saw this murder as a timely opportunity to end this particular line of hutagts once and for all, assuring the public that they were putting an end to a "loathsome and brutal line" of incarnate monks.

Meanwhile, Jintu Gonchig rode the horse Boriv Kheer back across the Gobi and returned to Gobi Mergen Van Hoshuu, only to find his monastery in ruins. Manchu troops had burnt Khashant Khiid to the ground and chased away the monks – retribution for the murder of the Mongol prince. Jintu had lost his spiritual leader and his sanctuary but was not deterred from his mission. Despite the decree laid down by his Manchu minders, he was determined to find the next incarnation in Outer Mongolia. His search would last seven years.

*   *   *

There is a legend about what became of the spirit of the Fourth Noyon Hutagt following his death. According to the tale, the mandala deity Yansang Yidam found the ger of a Gobi princess and revolved around her home for some time, hoping to be reborn from her womb. One night, the princess dreamed that she had given birth to a beautiful baby. Everyone who saw the child found wisdom, intellect and knowledge in his face. The lamas came to the princess and worshipped the woman who gave birth to such a wonderful child. They called her Ekh Dagina, "Dakini Mother."

The following day, the princess described the dream to her family and friends. Day after day the story of her dream grew haughtier, infuriating the spirit that revolved around the top of the ger. Although increasingly disenchanted with the candidate, the spirit did not give up entirely and continued to observe the goings-on.

The princess however, was rapidly attracting bad karma with her haughty behavior and failed to become pregnant. Lamas were brought into her ger to chant prayers for her pregnancy. Yansang Yidam watched all this from the wooden ring at the top of the ger. The inexperienced lamas, however, did more harm than good. Their abhorrent skills and clumsy prayers insulted the spirit. As the ceremony reached its zenith, bells rang out and drums were beaten. A trumpet sounded with an ear-piercing shrill and the horrified spirit collapsed into the ashes of the fire. Disgusted, Yansang Yidam fled to the countryside to search for an honest and clear womb, and the haughty princess failed to become pregnant.

*　*　*

We can better appreciate the origin of the 'dissatisfied spirit' legend once we learn more about Danzan Ravjaa's biological parents. In contrast to Ekh Dagina, Ravjaa's parents were poor beyond comprehension. They were the poorest of the Gobi poor, unable even to afford a proper ger, instead living in an *ovokhoo* (a tent with no support roof). Their worldly possessions included the clothes on their back and a solitary horse. The father, called Dulduit (of the Dorvod minority), had been a wandering minstrel, and perhaps a trained lama. He had recently been in the East Sunit region (near modern Shilingol) when he met his bride-to-be, a woman named Majikhan. As husband and wife they lived among other poor nomads and earned a pittance by begging or through laboring jobs when these were available. They were poor but honest and hard-working.

In his book *Trails to Inmost Asia*, explorer George Roerich described a typical band of nomads that must have been comparable to Danzan Ravjaa's parents.

"There seems to be a perceptible difference between the type of Mongols of the grass country of northern Mongolia, and that of the Mongol nomads dwelling in the Gobi, south of the Hangai Mountains and north of the Mongolian or Desert Altai. The northern Khalkha Mongol is stronger in build and is generally better dressed, being fond of bright colored silks and cloth. The nomads of the barren country round the Gobi Altai are often of inferior physique and smaller in stature, as if the unfavorable conditions of their life in the desert had checked their physical development. The crowd that surrounded our cars was poorly dressed; some wore old rags, others dirty sheepskins, worn over their bare skins… Their long unkempt tresses of black hair gave the company a wild look."[13]

Returning to the legend, this poor yet honest pair must have been attractive to the spirit that had just fled the home of Ekh Dagina. Content with its discovery, the spirit became part of Majikhan's first and only son, whom the couple named Ravjaa. It is said that when Dulduit received this baby into his scarf, he momentarily 'radiated light,' which, as Pozdneyev noted, was a characteristic trait for the birth of a huvilgan.

* * *

Ravjaa is a Tibetan word for "spreading out or blossoming." The exact time, date and place of Ravjaa's birth are open to debate. Some researchers suggest he was born at noon on Christmas Day, 1803, while others argue it was between 10am and 11am on January 8, 1804. The latter date is the more likely.

The birthplace is considered to be Dulaan Khar (Warm Blackness), in Gobi Mergen Van Hoshuu, a region which has alluring areas named Tooroigon Togol (Wild Boar Grove), Hulangiin Shand (Wild Ass Pond), Suvragiin Hailaas (Elm Stupa) and Zagiin Shugui (Saxaul Bush). Danzan Ravjaa's birthplace (modern-day Zuunbayan sum) is now considered a holy site – a monument was erected in 1988 and herders respect it by not placing their gers there.

After giving birth, so the story continues, Dulduit's wife grew hungry. Mongol custom dictates that a woman should eat fresh meat soup after she has given birth. Dulduit wandered off in search of food and encountered a traveling camel breeder named Tumor who was employed by an aristocrat. Tumor gave Dulduit the shinbone of a camel, which contained excellent fresh marrow. This was considered an auspicious sign and Dulduit believed he had received a special baby.

Dulduit, Majikhan and baby Ravjaa stayed near Dulaan Khar for three years. But the area was not safe, especially for a child. There was little protection from the sun and wind, not to mention the large number of snakes in the area.

In 1805 they moved to Örgön sum and it was in this year that Ravjaa's mother died of illness, leaving Dulduit alone with his two-year-old child.[14]

The year 1807 brought a *zud* – the Mongolian term for severe winter. It was an especially hard time for Dulduit and his son as they sought shelter with whatever family would house them. Exposure to the freezing cold and blizzards had a tremendous effect on Ravjaa. He grew up strong and resistant to pain and suffering. The father and son endured the misery of hunger and homelessness until an even greater tragedy struck – that summer a wolf killed Dulduit's only horse at a place called Horogiin Kheer. Seeking revenge, Dulduit waited for three days by the corpse of the horse with his crude flintlock gun. The wolf did not return and years later Ravjaa mentions the incident in his biography as a lesson about fate, vengeance and the relationship between man and beast.

*   *   *

A series of 'mystical' events then occurred that led local people into believing that Ravjaa was the reincarnation of the Fourth Noyon Hutagt. In one of these incidents Ravjaa and his father met a family that was packing up their belongings, preparing to move to new pastures. The family had no time to help the beggar pair. The woman of the ger handed Ravjaa a few scraps of food, but the boy was glaring at the greasy pot, just left over from a hot meal. Upon seeing this, the woman told him to lick the pot, if he were really that hungry.

As Ravjaa ate the leftovers, one arrogant family member said if Ravjaa were so desperate for food, he ought to lick both sides of the pot. Little Ravjaa, never one to back down from a challenge, grasped the iron cauldron and 'miraculously' turned it inside out. With the greasy innards of the pot now on the outside, Ravjaa proceeded to lick it clean, and asked his host if he had performed the task correctly. The amazed family immediately stopped their work and organized a feast in honor of the magical boy.[15]

Another childhood tale describes how Ravjaa reclaimed the knife and fire starter, which once belonged to the fourth incarnate, Jamyn Oidov Jampts. In their wanderings, Ravjaa and his father heard from others that a high-ranking Manchu juntung was traveling from Peking to Uliastai, a military outpost where a large division of soldiers was stationed. Because the caravan was passing nearby, Ravjaa insisted upon visiting the juntung. Dulduit agreed and they set off for the camp on a borrowed horse.

On reaching the camp, Dulduit asked the tent guard if he and his son could visit the juntung. The disapproving guard turned them away but little Ravjaa was adamant and shouted, "No event is complete in just one lifetime! I would like to speak with the juntung about my previous life!" The boy's sharp tongue surprised the guard but still he resisted. The juntung heard the commotion outside and invited Ravjaa to enter his tent. Dulduit kowtowed before the juntung but Ravjaa refused to give due respect.

"You have my knife and fire starter," he blurted out.

The juntung, taken aback, asked him to wait and left the tent. He returned with a package, unraveled the cloth and revealed the old silver knife and fire starter given to him by the Fourth Noyon Hutagt. Ravjaa touched the objects lovingly and thanked the juntung for returning 'his' belongings.

The juntung was shocked at hearing this but as a man of honor he promised to keep his silence and not harm the young incarnate.

*   *   *

While there are other myths about Ravjaa's childhood, one of the few events believed to be based on actual fact occurred during his seventh year. It was at this time that Ravjaa and his father joined an autumn feast, hosted by a family of wealthy herders. Because of their low rank in society, the pair was assigned a place on the floor near the door of the ger, traditionally the least respected area, usually reserved for children.

The feasting began and the people who had crowded into the tent were satisfied with the massive quantities of food and drink. As the celebration continued a cloudburst erupted overhead and raindrops pelted the tent. Much to the surprise and shock of the guests, the only section of the ger that leaked was the honored northern end where the most important people sit, including the head of the household. The visitors watched with horror as the less-honorable south end of the ger remained dry while the contemptuous host was soaked and humiliated.

"Why are these raindrops not falling on the heads of that ragged pair?" the host said angrily, pointing to Dulduit and his son. In response, Ravjaa composed a song, 'The Heavenly Sky,' or *Hurmast Tenger*. The first two stanzas are what he sang at the time and the following verses were added later.

> Heaven is complete
> Let's hold and enjoy eight magic feasts
> When clouds appear and the time of rain comes
> Where is the difference between the altar and the door?
> When the activities cease and the time of death comes
> What is the difference between old and young?
>
> When you plant a 'moilor' tree
> A snake and poison will come from the tree
> When you make friends with a bad person

You will learn bad things from them

When you plant a spreading tree
From each branch the fruits will come
When you have friendship with a good person
Brightness and wisdom will appear

Even though there are many heavenly stars,
The brightest ones are only one or two.
Even though there are many earthly creatures,
The wisest ones are only one or two.

They say that cold weather brings a chilly wind,
And that the ravine plants will revive
When you are happy.

Talk about unhappiness produces unhappiness
Zee Zee-hoo, zen vaiduu ze (have mercy), three saints[16]

The historian Walther Heissig writes that we can't necessarily assume a seven-year-old created this poem out of the blue. It's more likely that Ravjaa was using already existing phrases and rhymes taught to him by his father. Because the song has Shamanic overtones, it may have been derived from very old phraseology. Note this old Shamanic saying: "She is inflicted with an infectious disease, (to cure her) what is the difference between the lama and laymen (doctor)?" Or: "If one is afflicted with an infectious disease, what is the difference between old and young?"[17]

While his host must surely have been offended, the other guests in the ger were secretly impressed with Ravjaa's creativity and his ability to reference karma and Shamanic philosophy. Some joked that he must be a reincarnated saint, perhaps even the Fifth Noyon Hutagt! They were more right than they knew.

*   *   *

The eventual meeting between Ravjaa and Jintu Gonchig occurred in the snake year, 1809. Jintu had been traveling across the countryside for several years, interviewing young boys as he went, but had not yet found a child who he believed was the true incarnation of his former mentor.

It is said that Jintu Gonchig first identified Ravjaa during a summer feast at Tsagaan Tsav (modern day Mandakh sum), an area of natural beauty that is littered with petrified trees. At this festival, Jintu came upon Ravjaa and proceeded to question the boy in the typical fashion. Certain answers and signs immediately caught his attention. For example, Ravjaa identified a collection of Jintu's objects as his own, including a jade cup and a string of rosary beads once owned by the Fourth Noyon Hutagt.

Both of these items are now on display at the Danzan Ravjaa Museum. The rosary, created by the First Noyon Hutagt, contains 108 beads fashioned from the skulls of 108 skilled lamas. Each is inlaid with silver, gold and lapis lazuli. Making a rosary from human skulls was not unusual; as the beads are turned, the knowledge of the deceased lama helps to propel the prayer. Buddhist monks typically used other parts of the human body for creating their religious paraphernalia. The ganlin horn, a type of trumpet, was traditionally made from the femur of a 16-year-old virgin girl. Lamas' skulls were used to produce drinking cups and double-sided ritual drums. To drink from the skull of a well-versed lama is said to acquire his knowledge.

But most impressive was Ravjaa's claim that Jintu's horse was also his. Just as Jamyn Oidov Jampts had predicted, the horse from the Peking market connected them in the next life, a classic mark of Asian storytelling. Jintu had no doubt that this six-year-old was the incarnation he had sought for so long, and he brought him to Ongiin Gol monastery (modern-day Saikhan Ovoo sum, Dundgobi Aimag) for his enthronement.

En route to the Ongiin Gol monastery, Ravjaa passed through Tusheet Zasag Hoshuu, where he met an aristocrat, Toin Puntsag. The nobleman invited young Ravjaa into his tent to meet his mentally disturbed younger sister. Legend states that Ravjaa cured her ailment with his touch. In exchange for the miracle, the nobleman gave Ravjaa a black horse, which he rode to the enthronement ceremony. The living Buddha of Ongiin Gol Monastery, Ishdonilhudev Rimpoche, welcomed Ravjaa when he finally reached the temple.

Ravjaa's procession and coronation was, presumably, a widely celebrated and official event. There are no detailed descriptions of this particular enthronement, but according to Pozdneyev, every hutagt and huvilgan was given, quite literally, the royal treatment. Typically, a living Buddha would stay with his own family until the age of five or six. On an appointed day the child would be escorted in a long, colorful and slow parade to the monastery. The young huvilgan was seated upon his throne, presented with silk scarves and ceremonial ornaments, and sung a hymn of praise.

A shower of gifts from the lamas and laypeople followed. When Pozdneyev met the huvilgan of Orombo Monastery, he recorded that at ordination the boy received in total 1,540 horses, 800 cows, and over 1,000 sheep. Other gifts included gold and silver icons, animal pelts, silk, riding horses, a furnished ger and special embroidered wardrobes for each season of the year.[18] Following the ceremony, a feast and *naadam* (sports festival) was usually held.

Ravjaa's ordination was unique in that he was not actually called the Fifth Noyon Hutagt. The lamas, Ishdonilhudev Rimpoche and Jintu Gonchig, still feared the imperial order that banned this title.

Therefore, rather than calling him the Fifth Noyon Hutagt they granted him the title of Avshaa Gegeen, which had been held by a recently deceased lama named Navaan Agramba Tsorj.

For this reason Ravjaa began his monastic life officially recognized in Peking as "The incarnation of Avshaa," although the Mongol lamas privately knew him as the Fifth Noyon Hutagt.

When the ordination ceremony was complete, the peasant boy who had once begged for scraps of food was elevated to a status higher than any other in the desert and revered as His Holiness the Princely Saint, Lord of the Gobi.

3

INCIDENTS OF YOUTH

The restrictions of the monasteries must have been a great inconvenience to Ravjaa, who had never before experienced orders and regulations. As a peasant boy with a sharp tongue and healthy disrespect for authority, one can only guess what sort of trouble he caused for his minders. His worldview, one developed from both the sorrow of poverty and the love of his parents, must have seemed negative and cynical, but also sensitive. These troubled emotions were soon brought forth with pen and paper at hand and as Ravjaa grew older his talents as a songwriter and artist became more apparent.

Ravjaa's Buddhist studies took him to different monastic institutions in both Outer and Inner Mongolia. His father, however, was not so fortunate; Ravjaa's minders sent him away so that the young prodigy could tend more closely to his studies. Legend says that Dulduit was given a small pension to survive with, but this did not last long and he soon returned to his life of song and aimless wanderings. Dulduit died a pauper nine years later.

Having finished with Dulduit, it is important to mention several points about Ravjaa's parents. Firstly, there is reason to believe that

"Dulduit" was only a nickname. Later in life Ravjaa sometimes ended his compositions and poems by signing his name: "The son of Ulziit has just screamed." Dulduit was probably a moniker he picked up from his years as a beggar. A *dulduichin* was a person who attracted an audience with a bell, and then sang songs or read prayers in exchange for money or kind. Dulduit was probably a shortened form of dulduichin.

Furthermore it's possible that Ulziit was not Ravjaa's father at all but actually his mother and the stories about Ravjaa wandering around the desert with his father have lost their accuracy to time. This theory was first proposed by the scholar Ts. Damdinsuren, who pointed out that nowhere in Ravjaa's biography does he mention his father, although he writes 'Dulduit my mother' several times. Further, Ravjaa often dedicated poems to his mother, but never his father, who only seems to be mentioned in the last poem he would ever write. Damdinsuren considers that it is only through oral tradition and myth-making that people came to believe Dulduit was the father.

It is also possible that an error occurred when monks read the original biography. Therefore 'ejee' (mother) became 'ajaa' (father). Further evidence was identified by the Czech writer Marta Kiripolska who cites a quote from one of the biographies on Ravjaa.

"Even if I am a man who has (much knowledge of) the Dharma, I called the learned teachers and other lamas to perform religious services when my mother Dulduit died on the second day of the new moon of the first summer month of the snake year (assumed 1821), because a living being has nothing more precious than a mother, and she is as (difficult) to find as a star by daylight and because there is no better way (to perform) filial piety for (one's) gracious mother than (to help her achieve) Buddha (hood)."[19]

Because Ravjaa recorded this after he had entered the monastery, the quote discredits the myth that his mother died shortly after his birth. If the quote is accurate, then it seems that the many stories about Ravjaa's father were in fact about his mother.

*   *   *

The holiest city in northern Mongolia was of course the capital Huree (Urga) and Ravjaa was obligated to go there from a young age. In 1812, his minders at Ongiin Gol sent a request to Huree for an audience with the Fourth Bogd Gegeen, making an offering of 1,000 silver *lang*, along with valuable images of the Buddha. The application was accepted and Ravjaa was led north across the Gobi in a richly adorned caravan to the Bogd's winter residence. The trip took around five days.

On this occasion the Bogd Gegeen gave Ravjaa the Tibetan Buddhist spiritual name Lobsang Tenzin Rabgya, which in Mongolian pronunciation became Lobson Danzan Ravjaa. This became shortened to Danzan Ravjaa in common use.

In addition to a silver cup and a special *khadak* (silk scarf), the Bogd also allowed Ravjaa the honor of sitting on top of five *olbok* (a small square carpet) during religious ceremonies, signifying his status as an incarnate lama.

Ravjaa's early studies included a trip to Peking where he was interviewed by a variety of spiritual leaders, including a high-ranking Chinese monk named Yung-ho Kung.[20]

Legend says that the Fourth Panchen Lama (the seventh in the modern Chinese way of counting, see appendix) was in Peking at the time and met Ravjaa. He interviewed the young boy to determine his legitimacy as an incarnate lama and when asked to describe his family, Ravjaa called his mother a swan, a symbol that he would mention more frequently in his writings years later. The Panchen Lama was so impressed by the boy's answers that he became convinced that Danzan Ravjaa was indeed a living Buddha and should be treated like one. Meanwhile, the emperor had gotten wind that an incarnation of the Fourth Noyon Hutagt had entered his city and put an arrest order out on the boy. Attempts to have him eliminated were subsequently thwarted by a defiant Panchen Lama, with help from an appeal from the Dalai Lama.

Danzan Ravjaa's initial studies were conducted at the desert monastery of Ongiin Gol, where he had been enthroned. Here he was given basic teachings on Buddhist philosophy and practice, and was required to memorize the standard Buddhist liturgical texts. He was introduced to both Sanskrit and Tibetan literature and required to memorize the songs of Tibetan writers.

Ravjaa's studies, however, did not proceed as smoothly as his instructors would have hoped. Ongiin Gol lamas noted that he was not particularly attentive. Furthermore, he often ran away from the monastery to hide out with livestock breeders. Having grown up in rural areas, he no doubt had a particular affinity with them.

During one of these legendary escapes from the monastery, Ravjaa came upon a woman who was milking her cows. Meanwhile, a large brown bull was bucking about and constantly pestering her. The woman grew frustrated and, upon seeing young Ravjaa, ordered him to hold the bull.

Ravjaa's attempts to control the beast were unsuccessful. He was simply too small. Seeing this, the woman mumbled that Ravjaa was an ignorant and weak boy. Then, suddenly, the bull stopped kicking altogether and stood motionless by the ger.

Ravjaa remained at the ger for the night and, when it was time to sleep, the woman gave him only some tattered rags as bedding. Her small daughter took pity on Ravjaa and offered him her mattress and blanket.

The next morning the woman of the ger went outside and noticed that the bull was still motionless. The shaggy beast was pushed, pulled and smacked, but remained as still as stone. The hosts realized that Ravjaa must have cast a spell on the bull in return for the mistreatment he had received. They fell to their knees before him and asked for forgiveness.

"You should be kind to all people without prejudice, and that includes the poor and orphans," said Ravjaa. "Now you should give clothes and food to seven poor lamas to repent for your bad conduct."

Before departing, Ravjaa gave the kind daughter a silk scarf and predicted, "You will have a happy life, and will be the mother of three wonderful boys." As Ravjaa left, the old bull started to move and meandered over to the other cows grazing in the field.[21]

* * *

Young huvilgans spent much of their time with the old masters. It was a rare event that huvilgans were allowed to see other children, let alone play with them. Frolicking was discouraged and naughty behavior reprimanded. The older monks taught new recruits the fundamentals of Buddhism as well as other subjects including history, astronomy and literature. Creative skills were developed through drawing and modeling with clay. Pozdneyev relates that the wistful old monks also told them about their past lives, what the former incarnates owned, what they studied, where they traveled and what miracles they performed.

While this may have been a part of Ravjaa's early education, he was also exposed to art, music and chess, especially after he reached the age of 11, when he was allowed more freedom to move about the monastery and interact with others. According to the typical education given to a novice lama, he is likely to have received six hours of Buddhist lessons per day.

Ravjaa, it is said, had a particular affinity for languages and was given instruction in Tibetan, Mandarin, Mongolian and Manchu. Other stories suggest he also learned a few words of Russian and English from explorers, traders and travelers.

In 1817, at the age of 14, Ravjaa left Ongiin Gol and was sent to Alasha (Ālāshàn) and Ulaanchab in Inner Mongolia for continued studies. He was trained at Badgar Choilin süm (Chinese: Wudang Zhao) for three years (possibly five) and received an education in rhetoric and disputation. It was during this time that he took the *getsul* vows of a novice monk. The vows granted him permission to publicly perform spiritual works. He began accepting visitors for spiritual consultations and blessings, and was permitted to lead Buddhist rites. He was also considered old enough to perform divinations and prayer healings.

By 1822, now in his 19th year, he completed his basic Buddhist training and began the construction of his first temple, the Labrang Süm, built in the Hanggin Banner of the Ordos region (not to be confused with the more famous Labrang Monastery at Xiahe in Gansu province). He founded at least one more temple in the year 1823. [22]

At this young and impressionable stage in his life, Alasha must also have had a considerable influence on his creative talents. Tsam mask dancing, Chinese opera and folk songs were the seeds of his early writings. Ravjaa studied the poetry of Tibetan writers such as Rongbo Galdan Gyamtso (1607-1677) and perhaps read the songs of love and wine ascribed to the sixth Dalai Lama, who had also spent many years in the Alasha area.

In his early years Danzan Ravjaa met several times with the spiritual head of Doloon Nuur, the Fourth Janjiya Hutagt (1787 -1846), an important leader of the Gelugpa Buddhists. The two became close friends, as well as mentor and disciple. It's likely that the Janjiya Hutagt had significant spiritual influence on Ravjaa, encouraging him to follow the Gelugpa faith as well as the Nyingma tradition.

Ravjaa made several trips to Doloon Nuur (Chinese: Duolun) through the course of their relationship. On one such trip, in 1825, he arrived with two consorts and 100 of his own disciples for the purposes of making herbal medicines. [23]

Doloon Nuur is located just 250 miles north of Peking and not far from the site of Khublai Khan's summer capital Xanadu (Shangdu). Nowadays it is an unremarkable town whose population of 100,000 people is comprised almost exclusively of Chinese traders and peasants, with hardly a lama among them. A flat and sprawling mass of concrete and brick buildings, it is surrounded on all sides by fields of hay and vegetables. Although nondescript, it has certainly improved since the days when the Abbé Huc visited the city in 1842. He described it extensively:

"Toloon-Noor is not a walled city, but a vast agglomeration of hideous houses, which seem to have been thrown together with a pitchfork. The carriage portion of the streets is a marsh of mud and putrid filth, deep enough to stifle and bury the smaller beasts of burden that not infrequently fall within it, and those carcasses remain to aggravate the general stench; while their loads become the prey of the innumerable thieves who are ever on the alert.

Yet despite the nastiness of the town itself, the sterility of its environs, the excessive cold of its winter, and the intolerable heat of its summer, its population is immense, and its commerce enormous. Russian merchandise is brought hither in large quantities by way of (Khiakhtia). The Tartars bring incessant herds of camels, oxen and horses, and carry back in exchange tobacco, linen and tea… The trade of Toloon-Noor is mostly in the hands of men from the provinces of Shansi… In this vast emporium, the Chinese invariably make fortunes, and the Tartars are invariably ruined. Toloon-Noor, in fact, is a sort of great pneumatic pump, constantly at work in emptying the pockets of the unlucky Mongols." [24]

In its heyday, Doloon Nuur was famed for its craftsmen and ironworkers. Huge bronze statues were created here and sent to monasteries in Tibet and Mongolia. The Abbé Huc – who had a bronze statue of Jesus Christ cast here – describes seeing a train of six camels leaving the city laden with parts of a Buddhist statue to be assembled in Lhasa for the Dalai Lama. Huree likewise received a fine Buddhist image from Doloon Nuur, sent across the Gobi Desert in seven parts. The statue was placed in the Maidari Temple, which was once part of Zuun Huree, but which no longer exists.

It is most likely that Ravjaa's studies were conducted at the Shar

Süm (Yellow Temple), the largest temple complex in the city. Sadly, the Shar Süm no longer exists: according to a local curator, it was completely destroyed in 1945 by the Soviet Red Army during the final throes of WWII.[25] We are left, however, with a description of the temples, provided by Pozdneyev who visited the city in 1892 (or 1893).

> "The facades and architecture of these temples struck me as strongly reminiscent of the assembly hall in the Khalka Amarbayasgalant, except that the latter is made of wood, while the Doloon Nuur temples are of masonry and are ornamented in an incomparably more delicate, elegant, and lavish style than the Amarbayasgalant one. The designs of their cornices, the abundance of the most fantastic sculpture, marvelous reliefs, and the graceful tapering, polished, and gilded columns – all this is really strikingly lovely and causes no small wonder in any beholder."[26]

Dating from 1691, the Yellow Temple, at its height, housed several thousand monks studying the arts and astronomy. Emperor Kangxi commissioned this temple as a gift for Mongolia's spiritual leader Zanabazar. An earlier complex on the same site had been destroyed by fire, and the construction of the Yellow Temple was funded with 120,000 silver coins given by the Manchu government, as part of a scheme to promote unity between Inner and Outer Mongolia. The Manchus had recently subdued the latter and the Yellow Temple was designated as a symbolic intermediary between the two Mongol states. The monastery grew in importance in 1732 after the second Bogd Gegeen of Mongolia fled violence in Huree and was taken there for his own safety. By that time some 3,000 lamas were living in the monastery and another 4,000 lived in the city itself. Money poured in as Doloon Nuur became a popular pilgrimage site.[27]

Although the Yellow Temple no longer exists, there still remains in Doloon Nuur the former residence of the Janjiya Hutagt. The buildings were located next to the Yellow Temple and it's likely that Danzan Ravjaa was a frequent visitor.

As well as delving into intensive Buddhist studies, Ravjaa also used Doloon Nuur as a staging point for visits to Peking. From Doloon Nuur, Ravjaa also made at least one pilgrimage with the Janjiya Hutagt to the holy mountain Wutai Shan, probably in the year 1825. Wutai was a favorite destination for Mongolian pilgrims who not only climbed the mountain but also prayed inside the famed "Mother Cave" close to the southern peak. Once inside the Mother Cave, pilgrims crawled through a small hole in the wall, thereby purifying their sins in an act of virtual rebirth. They passed through this "womb" with the assistance of a Chinese monk nicknamed "the midwife."[28] It's unlikely that Ravjaa was alone on this pilgrimage; in summer a constant stream of Mongols came to visit the mountain.

The sanctity of Wutai is said to have been the inspiration for Ravjaa's 12-verse poem 'Pure and Clear,' which was dedicated to his elder companion. It was one of Ravjaa's early masterpieces, and was followed by several other popular poems, including 'The Kite,' which was penned in 1826.

*   *   *

Although not nearly as in demand as the Bogd Gegeen, Danzan Ravjaa, even in his younger years, received a steady stream of visitors seeking his blessing. His popularity continued to grow as he transitioned from student to teacher, and the list of the devout seeking his counsel grew even longer.

When people of high rank or authority wanted an audience with a huvilgan, they at first needed to overcome a lengthy bureaucratic process. First a message was sent to the huvilgan, explaining in detail the purpose of the visit and the hour of arrival. The huvilgan, if he consented to the audience, then sent a letter of invitation.

On the day of the meeting, the monk and his visitor would meet outside the temple hall or meeting room, each giving a slight bow. Then began the difficult process of who should enter the room first, and once inside, where each was to sit. The person of highest rank entered first and sat at the northern part of the room. All this was done according to unwritten rules of rank. Chinese officials typically considered themselves of highest rank, an assumption that often incensed the Mongols. The huvilgan ranked under the Chinese. Lowest of all were the Mongol noblemen.

A meeting would typically begin with an exchange of greetings and pleasantries. Then all matters related to the visit were touched upon with the utmost of diplomacy. Formalities only lightened with the occasional draining of brandy or vodka bottles. In a ceremonial end to the meeting, the huvilgan presented a gift and blessing to his guest.

Common people did not need to go through such formal procedures. Their experience with the huvilgan, however, could hardly be deemed social. The devotee would silently enter the huvilgans' quarters and prostrate himself three times. The living Buddha would then give blessings by touching the pilgrim's head with his hands or a book. Satisfied and humbled, the worshipper would offer a prayer and then slip out of the room in silence. Some travelers described how the huvilgans would sometimes play practical jokes on the commoners who came for a blessing. Pozdneyev wrote about the monk with whom he stayed in Inner Mongolia:

> "(The Orombo Gegeen) was terribly bored by these admirers, and then instead of placing a holy book on the head of the praying person, he whacked them on the head with a sword, or even gave them a push with his foot, or filliped him on his pate. All this does not in the least offend the religious feeling of the Mongols; on the contrary the more eccentric the escapade, the more it makes the son of the steppes be thoughtful… If later in the life of that Mongol something important happened, the huvilgan's innocent prank will be given suitable signification by the lamas."[29]

A visit by a foreigner was always a pleasant surprise and gave the senior monks an opportunity to make inquiries about foreign lands and world affairs. Because of such contact the huvilgans, compared to other Mongols, were well informed. Russian visitors, compared to Chinese ones, were particularly well liked as they provided Mongolia's only window to the West. Such visits were also an opportunity for the monks to exchange valued gifts. Pozdneyev noted that most senior monks he visited possessed a variety of knick-knacks from Europe and elsewhere in Asia. Their shelves were filled with old watches, clocks, microscopes, globes and photographs – the classifying of which occupied much of their time.

* * *

As mentioned earlier, Danzan Ravjaa made extensive travels between the years of 1825 and 1827, making trips to Wutai Shan, Doloon Nuur, Peking and numerous monasteries in the border areas between Inner Mongolia and China proper. In fact the years between 1825 and 1836 were extremely busy ones for Danzan Ravjaa as he constantly traveled back and forth between Inner and Outer Mongolia, plus a few trips deeper into China. In the second half of 1827 his wanderings halted long enough to construct three monasteries in Outer Mongolia: Demchog, Ulaan Sakhosnii Khiid (named after his protector) and Sayan Tolai Khiid. His chosen location for the monasteries was the Galbaa Gobi region (modern Khanbogd sum, Ömnögov Aimag), an isolated desert area of jumbled red rocks and wind-raked plains. Construction of the monasteries lasted six years but when they were finished all became important centers of learning and spirituality. Collectively they were known as Gurvan Galbiin Khiid. Sadly, none survived the purges of the 1930s and only Demchog has seen recent attempts at restoration.

Ulaan Sakhosnii Khiid was the best known of the three and its remains can still be found today. The main temple was placed close to a cave. Brick walls enclosed the area between the rocky outer portion of the cave and the temple. Within this yard, Ravjaa built an artificial lake and stream with artificial rock 'mountains.' It must have resembled, in some distant way, a Japanese Zen garden. Danzan Ravjaa had at least one Japanese disciple, and it was possibly this student who designed the garden grounds. When a groundbreaking ceremony for the temples was held he invited hundreds of mothers (legends say 10,000) to the event and gave them seats of honor, as a way of publicly declaring his strong respect for women.

In 1829, after laying the groundwork for these buildings, Ravjaa returned to Inner Mongolia. For some months he roamed between monasteries in the Chahar region, eventually reaching Doloon Nuur, where he received the secular title Van Janan.

Despite his young age, Danzan Ravjaa was already regarded as an influential huvilgan as well as something of an eccentric character. He spent a good deal of his time writing poetry and watching opera. His first attempts to organize and direct theater probably began at this time. Most of all, he was clearly living up to his 'dogshin' moniker, with legendary displays of anger, frequent binges on alcohol and long disappearances into his door-less ger. It was around this time, in 1831, that he embarked on one of his more unusual projects, the excavation and renovation of Agui Süm (Cave Temple) in Alasha.

Today Agui Süm (also known as Lovonchimbu Süm) is a remote and almost deserted temple complex located about 110km northwest of modern Dengkou city in Inner Mongolia. One hundred years ago it was one of the biggest monasteries in Alasha and a popular pilgrimage destination for Mongols who came from as far away as Huree. Danzan Ravjaa is credited with having developed the monastery and its nearby cave complex.

According to local lore, the sanctity of the site stems from a visit by Padmasambhava in the year 774. Upon some investigation he found five dakini sisters in the caves and stayed to engage in tantric practices with them. Padmasambhava also subdued a demon, which he locked inside one of the caves. He left a footprint embedded in the rock as proof of his visit.

A boy named Zandari lived near the caves and Padmasambhava took it upon himself to make him a disciple. Years later Zandari returned to the cave and established a monastery. The actual foundation of the monastery probably dates to around the turn of the 18th century.

Ravjaa first arrived in 1831 when he was 28 years old. He stopped here en route to Amdo where he planned to make a pilgrimage to Kumbun Monastery.

"Hanqin" Pandita (pandita means scholar), the local huvilgan who presided over the monastery, welcomed Ravjaa to Agui Süm. As usual, Ravjaa had in tow a caravan of disciples and a healthy supply of alcohol. The sanctity of the caves moved Ravjaa greatly and following his departure to Amdo he started to plan a longer visit. He returned two years later and on this second trip brought with him a large quantity of Buddhist textbooks, tsam masks and a large statue of Padmasambhava. Ravjaa placed the statue inside the Padmasambhava cave (one of five at the site) and built a central Assembly Hall. The masks and books were likewise donated to the monastery. Finally, he "excavated" the cave temples, which likely means that he had them cleared of debris and deepened. The popularity of the hutagt meant that other pilgrims would follow, bringing with them sorely needed donation money.

A handful of Western, Russian and Japanese visitors also came to the monastery, leaving useful descriptions and accounts of the site. One Western traveler, French count Jacques de Lesdain, provided observations from his two-day visit in 1904. Of particular interest, he wrote of seeing a cart near the caves. He was told that pilgrims from Urga had used the cart to carry a statue of the Buddha. This may have been the cart used by Danzan Ravjaa when he came with the Padmasambhava statue, some 70 years earlier.[30]

* * *

Central to the story of Danzan Ravjaa is Khamaryn Khiid. Not only was it one of Ravjaa's prime monasteries but it also figured prominently in the research of this book as I made several trips to it starting in 2000. The buildings here were commissioned in 1820 to replace Khashant Khiid, which was closed by the authorities after the death of Jamyn Oidov Jampts.

The project had begun with an analysis of the best possible location for the new monastery. For this Ravjaa turned to his old guru the Janjiya Hutagt of Doloon Nuur Monastery. He also consulted a certain Doyod, an elderly monk and Gobi native who had a knack for locating water in the harsh desert. Together they crossed the harsh landscape of the Gobi in search of a suitable place for a new monastery.

At last they came to a place called Övör Hamar, which was marked by a stupa, and made habitable by a spring and a saxaul forest. A study was made of the area: trees were counted, water located and the terrain surveyed.

An extra in the story is one Khilenhormoi, a dark-skinned, muscular old cowboy-hermit who lived the area. Khilenhormoi was one of Mongolia's most notorious *Sain Er*, or highwaymen.

Crouched down in a hunting bunker, Khilenhormoi kept a wary eye on Danzan Ravjaa as the monk approached. Ravjaa liked the bunker and thought it would offer good protection for his temples against bandits. He also liked the look of Khilenhormoi. As a strong believer in the theory of yin and yang, Ravjaa was sure that his ornery exterior masked a kind and proud interior.

Ravjaa approached Khilenhormoi but the bandit only ignored Ravjaa and his companions. A bloody, dirty gazelle carcass was lying at his side, causing the lamas to turn away in disgust. Ravjaa was not deterred; he spoke kindly with Khilenhormoi and his magnetism cast a spell over the hardened cowboy. Khilenhormoi was soon hired by Ravjaa to work as a guard at the monastery.

After Ravjaa had selected the spot he set about digging wells in the surrounding area. One day he was surveying northwest of the monastery and announced that a new well would be dug at the top of a hill. One look at the dry rocky mound caused concern among Ravjaa's students who stated emphatically that no water could come from it. To which Ravjaa stated:

"If your head is pierced what things would come out? It's a natural law that strong and weak matter is found together. So where there are hard stones, there will be groundwater."

Ravjaa's students reluctantly dug, and after half a fathom, clear and cold water poured forth. Their faith restored in the hutagt, they erected a fence around the new well.

Another version of this story explains that, while standing by the Lavriin Temple of his monastery, Ravjaa took his bow and arrow – used in his tsam dances – and announced that wherever his arrow would land was the place where a new well would be dug. Sure enough his disciples found groundwater in the place where his arrow fell. Yet another version has it that the water sprung forth because salt water, used to clean the corpses of the third and fourth hutagts, had been poured on this spot.

Ravjaa proclaimed the water to be holy and said its properties could cure ailments of the teeth, eyes, blood, joints and liver. There were many customs associated with this spring: women were not allowed to mix the water, animals could not be brought there, the water could not be collected with a metal cup, and women could not go near it if they had any exposed wounds.

The spring was maintained until 1938, the year Khamaryn Khiid was destroyed. In 1970, while Buddhism was still outlawed in Mongolia, attempts made to restore the well all failed. Then in

1991, a year after Buddhism returned, two local people dug on the spot and struck the same cold water Ravjaa had found 150 years before. In the year 2000, a protective hexagonal structure was built around the spring to ensure the protection of its curative waters.

Khamaryn Khiid was comprised of four quarters: Zuun Huree, Baruun Huree, Tsokhon and Duinkhor. Ravjaa usually remained in the Zuun Huree area, which included the Lavriin temple, a library, and a school for young lamas. In Zuun Huree, a temple was built to house the remains of the fourth Noyon Hutagt, and later the sixth Noyon Hutagt would be interred here.

Baruun Huree contained the Givadiin Ravjaaliin temple-museum and a cooking area. The Duinkhor quarter held temples as well as the theater where Ravjaa staged his operas. At its height, the entire monastery contained 13 temples (with 22 chapels), two stupas and 11 smaller buildings. Nearly everyone at Khamaryn Khiid, monks and nuns included, lived in gers that circled the temples. It is said that there was room enough for a population of 500 monks and nuns.[31]

*   *   *

Danzan Ravjaa was a practical man. In his poem "By All Kinds of Things" he wrote:

> You have been born as a human being
> Don't do anything that is not necessary
> You have to pray to the very good deity 'Makhgal'
> Always think about good things for your society[32]

Through this verse and others like it seen in his poetry we know that Ravjaa was very much concerned about both the welfare of society and the need to accomplish tasks quickly and efficiently. His various projects were governed by both of these principles.

For example, he once asked his monks to build livestock stables, explaining that Buddhism would some day suffer and future generations would have more use for stables than monasteries.

It was said that the slow and apathetic work of the monks in building these stables infuriated Ravjaa. "We are building these stables for the future, don't you know this?" Ravjaa bellowed. "Why are you all so lazy? Do you think a world dependent on time is eternal?"

His cowering disciples asked, "You are leading this blessed work, so why do you say such harsh words?"

Ravjaa replied, "Nothing in this world is eternal, and human behavior will always change. And so Buddhism also changes – there are times when it has flourished and times when it has suffered. It will be the same in the future. So we must take advantage of this period of blessing and work hard to create things for the sake of our children. In the future, people will kick and destroy religion, but they will still need food. These stables will be a blessing for them."

The story shows, as does the verse from "By All Kinds of Things", that Ravjaa believed strongly in preparing his people for any eventualities.

It would appear that Ravjaa correctly predicted the fate of Buddhism in Mongolia, for a century later Communist forces went to great lengths to ensure the utter destruction of the enlightenment tradition.

The era of suffering for Mongolia's monks lasted 60 years, from the late 1920s to the late 1980s. Interestingly, the cycle of benevolent and malevolent periods for Buddhism as mentioned by Ravjaa can also last 60 years, or five cycles of the 12-year lunar calendar.

The re-emergence of Buddhism in Mongolia has, among many other things, allowed for a better understanding of Danzan Ravjaa. Before 1990, much of the known information regarding this historical figure was based upon myth. Understanding his life from a Buddhist perspective was difficult given the restrictions of the time. Researchers can now study his life from a more philosophical and religious point of view.

What they discovered was that Ravjaa was not debauched, as he had been so enthusiastically portrayed by the Communists, but to the contrary was a brilliant and creative genius, although somewhat eccentric.

The next chapter will explore Ravjaa's own unique and personal relationship with the Buddhist faith.

4

RAVJAA AND BUDDHISM

Altangerel, the curator of the Danzan Ravjaa Museum, has one artifact in his collection that he keeps under lock and key in his private office. It is a book with 108 pages, each one tied to the next so that it unfolds like an accordion. On each page is a crude line drawing of a man and woman in various sexual positions. The artwork is unspectacular and nothing like the complex color paintings that adorn the walls of monasteries. In comparison with the other artwork within the museum, these are rather amateurish. Still, Altangerel recognizes its obvious appeal and knows that if anything were to be stolen from his museum, it would be this book.

Alcohol and sex were fairly common in Mongolia's monasteries, particularly during Danzan Ravjaa's lifetime. The strict traditions of the Yellow School that prohibited these indulgences were unlikely to have ever been followed very closely.

However, Danzan Ravjaa's apparent addiction to both alcohol and sex must have seemed an extreme case, and was certainly enough to bring criticism from senior monks.

Perhaps Danzan Ravjaa engaged in very high levels of tantric practice and did not feel bound by the ordinary laws of Buddhism.

After a certain level of realization, the letter of the monk vows may have been overlooked. His poetry stresses virtue, morality and the bodhisattva vow and it is perhaps this vow that supersedes any other formal vows he might have taken.

He did not consider sex to be something dark or hidden and he did not forbid his disciples from engaging in sexual activities. In fact, he suggested they could learn from their sexual encounters, that these ideas could improve their meditation and assist in their ultimate goal of overcoming vice, which obstructs the path to enlightenment. He was possibly using tantric imagery, if not encouraging tantric yab/yum practice.

When he preferred to meditate, Ravjaa retreated to the Yalkhoi caves located near Khamaryn Khiid. Here the complex of "108 Caves for the 108 Students" is a series of niches in the volcanic rock, with the caves being set between dry wash ravines. They are named after the deity who protects them, Yalkhoi, who is often featured in paintings riding a red goat. Most caves here are nothing more than table-sized notches in the red walls, but one or two are big enough to fit a dozen huddled monks. The number 108 seems to be merely symbolic.

One cave in particular has a unique function. In reality it is more of an overhang than a cave. Pilgrims believe that crawling through this small passage purifies negative karmas collected over many lifetimes.

The promontory above the caves is called 'Offering Hill' and is so named for a legendary vulture that comes here to offer food – in the form of dead rodents – in exchange for spiritual protection from Yalkhoi.

Today the caves still contain Buddhist tokens: carved stones, silk scarves, bits of jewelry and coins. In the largest cavern, an altar bears a photo of the seventh Noyon Hutagt. These are not leftover relics from decades past; pilgrims still come here to pray and make offerings.

It was considered an honorable task for the monks of Khamaryn Khiid to perform the strict 108-day retreat at the caves. To begin this retreat, a monk would enter one of the tiny caves and allow his peers to seal him up behind a wall of bricks or stones. A small hole was left in the wall of the cave. One meal arrived each day in a wooden cup and once he had eaten the food, the monk turned the cup over and scraped the rim three times before pushing it outside again, thus making the cup shrink each day.

Every day the cup was returned with food but mid-way through the retreat it would have been scraped down to its wooden base. Without a cup to hold his food, the monk would simply fast for the remainder of his retreat.

After 108 days, the wall was knocked down and the monk brought out. It is said that just 12 monks from Khamaryn Khiid managed the entire 108 days.

After a few days of rest, monks would surround the successful retreatant and read sutras in his honor. Legends claim that 60 cartloads of sutras would be read. It was believed that the monk, so soon after his retreat, had gained extraordinary powers and would memorize all that was read to him.

Upon completion of the sutra reading, the monk was taken back to the sacred caves and asked to display his newfound abilities. A *purba* (small ritual dagger) was set on the ground about ten feet from the monk, who was encouraged to use the power of thought to raise it from the ground, make it turn in mid-air, and then make it fall back, point-first, into the earth. Anyone who could perform this feat was given special honors. However, there was no shame in failing this test. The monk would still advance in rank and be considered a worthy teacher.

Danzan Ravjaa completed his first meditation retreat in Ömnögov (possibly at one of his three monasteries at Gurvan Galbiin Khiid). According to legend, he needed no rest upon completion of his retreat and easily memorized the 60 cartloads of sutras that were read to him. When the time came to prove his skills, he not only lifted the purba, but also sent it flying into a nearby cliff. Today, locals can point out the marks in the rock wall caused by the flying purba.

"The monks from Khamaryn Khiid sat in the caves for days or weeks at a time. During their meditation they sent blood to circulate in their heads, giving them clarity of thought," explained D. Bold, the curator of the Sainshand History Museum. "But few people could pass this challenge. If they died in the caves their bones were left there. These bones added spiritual power to the caves."[33]

* * *

When not meditating, the monks used the caves as a place for philosophical discussions and debates on theories of Buddhism such as emptiness, a topic that writer and Zen teacher Philip Kapleau calls "the dynamic substream of all existence."

Danzan Ravjaa defined emptiness in a poem:

> Emptiness is the miracle
> Which has no shape
> No direction to go and come
> No color to identify
> No space to exist.[34]

He gives further examples:

> Expectations are empty
> And emotional pain is empty
> To succeed and to error are attributes of the mind
> God is the imagination of the mind
> And Erlig is the imagination of the mind
> Good and evil come from the mind
> And all emotions are empty
> Emptiness is the miracle of being[35]

Here Ravjaa suggests that the human mind, not anything tangible, is the source of superstition, gods, Erlig, and emotional pain. Therefore individuals, not an external being, have the power to destroy afflictions that haunt the mind. The poem is also a statement that all things are not inherently real in any ultimate sense.

To take one more example from Ravjaa's writings, consider the following poem, which explains that so-called opposites are merely concepts with no real basis.

> White and black are inseparable
> Good and bad are inseparable
> Yes and no are inseparable
> Above and below are inseparable
> Fast and slow are inseparable
> Happiness and suffering are inseparable
> Everything has an opposite, but no reality, just names[36]

Emptiness also includes visible and seemingly tangible objects, including sunlight. One day Ravjaa asked his students if sunlight was empty. Of course, they said, having never known sunlight to contain solid properties.

Ravjaa then held up a snuff bottle and placed it over a sunbeam that was shining through a hole in the top of the cave. He released the snuff bottle but it seemed to be suspended in mid-air on the beam of light. Here Danzan Ravjaa shows to his students that all of their expectations, thoughts, assumptions and perceptions are empty.

Consider a wall as another example. If Ravjaa substituted the word 'air' for 'wall,' could he push his hand through the wall of the cave? As the story goes, Ravjaa put his snuff bottle away and proceeded to push his hand into the solid cave wall.

*   *   *

Danzan Ravjaa may have received substantial education in Buddhism, having been instructed by the most advanced teachers, but according to some European accounts, most Mongol monks and lamas of the 19th century had little more than a basic grounding. Being geographically distant from the great religious centers of Tibet, Nepal and Bhutan, Mongolia's Buddhist educational system suffered from its isolation. The Abbé Huc described his encounter with the lamas of Doloon Nuur:

> The Lamas appeared to us persons of very limited information… When we asked them for some distinct clear, positive idea of what they meant, they were always thrown into utter embarrassment, and stared at one another. The disciples told us that their masters knew all

about it; the masters referred us to the omniscience of the Grand Lamas; the Grand Lamas confessed themselves ignorant, but talked of some wonderful saint, in some Lamasery at the other end of the country: *he* could explain the whole affair... When we expounded to them the truths of Christianity, they never discussed the matter; they contented themselves with calmly saying, "Well, we don't suppose that our prayers are the only prayers in the world."[37]

Many Western travelers who visited Mongolia before the Communist revolution commented negatively on the state of the monasteries. The accounts of the German traveler Otto Manchen-Helfen, the writings of the Scottish missionary James Gilmour, and even the Russian Przewalski are in the same vein in this respect.

The views of these visitors, most of whom were Christian missionaries, tend to fall in line with the most arrogant beliefs prevalent in 19th-century Europe. It is therefore necessary to question the judgments of their observations.

There are no real journalistic accounts of what Danzan Ravjaa's monasteries were like when he was alive. It is probable that life in them was much the same as in the other Mongolian monasteries. However, there is no doubt that he drove his monks hard in both scriptural study and the practice of meditation, and strongly encouraged both the arts and social service.

That said, one could also surmise that Ravjaa might have agreed with these travelers and missionaries in some respects, for he was always quick to offer his criticism of hypocrisy, immorality and social justice wherever he found it. One of his best-known poems, entitled *Shame and Shame* (Ichig Ichig), does just that, and provides us with a humorous condemnation of society at every level. We will see that poem in the following chapter.

5

Mongolia in the 19th Century

"You kill, kill. And make dried meat.
You call the living beings the poor ones. Oh World!
You take and take the human belongings with deception
But you have a dislike for gain, oh World!"
Danzan Ravjaa[38]

W as Danzan Ravjaa speaking about his own society when he wrote these words? Was he reflecting on the poverty and injustice of his times?

The 19th century was something of a low point in Mongolia's 800-year history. The country was riddled by debt, ruled by a petty aristocracy, and overseen by the Manchus who implemented a divide-and-conquer strategy.

Most records from the 19th century are not neatly classified historical documents. Too much was destroyed by the Communist cultural purges to enable us to gather a complete picture of things, at least at the present time. We have few letters, memoirs or journalistic accounts, since there was no established system to allow for formalized documentation.

Society in 19th-century Mongolia was more stratified than it had been in previous generations. Manchu administrators granted titles to strengthen the aristocracy, splitting the country between rich and poor, and creating a divide that they hoped might prevent alliances and rebellion. The lay people were separated into two main classes: the *albutu* (commoner) and the *taij* (nobility).

The taij, wrote the historian Sir Henry Howarth, were not shy of exercising their power.

> "The Taidjs or Noyans have a dominant authority over their subjects. They can make or unmake their fortunes; can have them bastinadoed or have their noses or ears or hands cut off, but they seldom put them to death (except secretly), since that is contrary to the Lama religion."[39]

However, Howarth also noted that the aristocracy and commoners were not segregated.

> "The power of the nobles is implicitly recognized by their dependants and their orders strictly obeyed, and on meeting a noble a peasant will go down on his knees to do him honor. Their intercourse otherwise is, however, perfectly friendly. On rising from their knees the ordinary Mongols will sit down beside their chief, discuss affairs with him, and smoke pipes together. The chief, however, can appropriate their sheep or beat them without there being any appeal to a higher chief."[40]

Although the aristocracy of 19th-century Mongolia seemed content to play by Manchu rules, I can identify one exception. The Tsetsen Khaan Aimag prince named Togtokhtor, or To-Van, was a uniquely progressive force in his day. To-Van built schools, temples and monuments with the tax money that he collected. Considered a generous visionary and philanthropist, he was a contemporary of Danzan Ravjaa and may have been influenced by him (there is no record of a meeting, though letters may have been exchanged).

To-Van traveled widely in China and studied the life of his sedentary southern neighbors. He brought back to his homeland craftsmen and other skilled workers to educate his subjects. He also brought back new ideas on how to efficiently run his territory. Rather than remaining dependent on Chinese traders for goods, he encouraged people to work independently and become self-sufficient. He urged his countrymen to collect nuts, fruit, wild grain, mushrooms and onions. During his rule, agriculture, hunting and fishing increased, gold mines opened, water mills were built, salt and soda were collected, and workshops were made to create building materials. He was frugal and encouraged his subjects to save their goods and work hard. In a book of handy tips for the people of his banner he wrote, "Wives ought to work continuously, educating their children, doing sewing or other work, dealing with the cattle stalls and so on, only eating and drinking when their husband comes home."

To-Van gave practical instructions to herders for livestock breeding and care, on how to build winter shelters, repair saddles and gers, and protect animals during natural disaster. Like Danzan Ravjaa, he was an aficionado of culture. He promoted Buddhist art, commissioned a huge statue of Chenraisig on the banks of the Khalkh Gol (it is still there today), and opened an arts college with separate schools for theater, painting, sculpture and music. He also opened an elementary school and personally designed the curriculum.

To-Van opposed Manchu rule and often came into conflict with his overlords. In such instances he was known for his cunning diplomacy. In one instance, a dispute arose over land rights that included a sacred hill. To-Van proposed to the Manchus that if he could cover the hill with one cattle hide it would be his. The Manchus agreed. To-Van then had the cattle hide cut into a long string, with which he circled the hill, thereby winning the contest.

*   *   *

Danzan Ravjaa would have been impressed with the changes happening during To-Van's rule. But the Fifth Hutagt was careful with the relations he had with Mongolia's aristocrats. He honored those princes who worked to improve life for Mongolia but was critical of aristocrats who took advantage of their titles or high rank. This is exemplified in a tale about a certain taij who came to Khamaryn Khiid on pilgrimage.

According to the story, Ravjaa was drinking vodka alone one night when the taij entered his ger. There in the tent were two chairs, two silver cups and a full bottle of *arkhi* (vodka), which seemed invitation enough for the taij to sit down. The taij had a bright and cheery demeanor, but Ravjaa, who had the power to determine the qualities of a man, saw trickery and deceit in his eyes. He considered this pilgrim unworthy of sharing his drink. Instead he mocked the visitor as a *badarchin* (wanderer) and drank incessantly without offering a drop to his guest.

The taij finally lost his patience and pleaded for a drink, at which Ravjaa demanded to know on what grounds he should give him his arkhi.

"I am from divine lineage and white bones," the taij said. "I have drunk arkhi since I was a child." A Mongol of 'white bones' is a person of high-ranking nobility.

Ravjaa, showing no respect to the class of the man before him, replied, "You may be of white bones, but I am a donkey. That is why I drink arkhi as if it were water. So go to your place of high aristocrats, drink your arkhi and feast." He waved the pilgrim out of his tent.

This story is a favorite in Mongolia as it again shows Ravjaa's disregard for the wealthy and the upper classes. The story also exemplifies his stubborn and bull-headed personality, not to mention his love of drink.

The story also states that Ravjaa could drink arkhi as if it were water, which indicates his yogic ability to drink as much as he liked without truly becoming intoxicated, a well-known ability of tantric masters. It was these traits that elevated Ravjaa to a special place in dismal 19th-century Mongolia; at a time of despair, here was a man who broke all the rules and gave his followers a greater sense of self-respect.

* * *

It seems certain that 19th-century Mongolia suffered considerably from poverty. Most of the country's money was in the hands of Chinese usurers, who maintained high interest rates on their loans and dominated the economy to their own advantage. In effect, the entire country was mortgaged to China for 200 years.

Poverty increased during Danzan Ravjaa's lifetime – in 1816 Tushet Khan Aimag was home to 13,666 people living in debt; that number rose to 17,752 by 1837.[41]

Most Mongols today blame the Manchus for reducing them to financial ruin during that period of their history. However, it is possible that the Mongolians themselves walked openly into the situation.

The Abbé Huc recorded his observations of trade between the Chinese and Mongols in the 1840s:

> "The commercial intercourse between the Tartars and the Chinese is revoltingly iniquitous on the part of the latter. So soon as Mongols, simple, ingenuous men, if such there be at all in the world, arrive in a trading town, where they are snapped up by some Chinese, who carry them off... to their houses, give them tea for themselves and forage for their animals, and cajole them in every conceivable way. The Mongols, themselves without guile and incapable of conceiving guile in others, take all they hear to be perfectly genuine, and congratulate themselves, conspicuous as they are of their inaptitude for business, upon their good fortune in thus meeting with brothers, *ahatou*, as they say, in whom they can place full confidence and who will undertake to manage their whole business for them...

> When once the Chinese has got hold of the Tartar, he employs him all the resources of the skilful and utterly unprincipled knavery of the Chinese character. He keeps them in his house, eating and drinking and smoking, one day after another, until his subordinates have sold all the poor man's cattle, or whatever else he has to sell, and brought for him the commodities he requires, at prices double and triple the market value. But so plausible is the Chinese, and so simple is the Tartar, that the latter invariably departs with the most entire conviction of

the immense philanthropy of the former, and with a promise to return, when he has other goods to sell, to the establishment where he has been treated so fraternally."[42]

Dependence grew on the Manchus not only for banking but also for the production of goods. Even the simplest items like metal pots, cloth, saddles and needles had to be imported or made in Chinese or Manchu owned shops.

Debtors were often subject to a beating for failing to pay off a loan. A common punishment included the placement of a cangue (wooden block) around the neck, where it might remain for up to two years. Another punishment was to tie up the debtor in a wet hide and leave him exposed to the elements. Whippings, beatings, and jailing were also commonplace. Jail cells usually consisted of a locked wooden coffin with a small hole cut into the side for air. It was this harsh treatment under Manchu rule that left leaders such as Danzan Ravjaa in utter dismay. In adulthood he found an outlet for his frustrations in his dramatic poetry, plays and operas.

As mentioned in the previous chapter, Ravjaa took great delight in criticizing inequalities wherever he encountered them. One of his poems which best exemplifies this is *Shame and Shame*. It is beloved by Mongols because it holds back nothing and avoids no targets in its swings. He even ends it by criticizing himself!

Oh, the elders who did not give charity, shame
Oh, the young ones. Dandified but not purified in their soul, shame
Oh, the wise, who lack devotion to learning, shame
Oh, the noble, who discriminates against his subjects, shame

Oh, the girl who nurses her man instead of her parents, shame

Oh, a statesman who abuses his power, shame

Oh, the pupil who does not learn the book but learns things rotten, shame

Oh, monks lacking meditation but shout for comfort, shame

Oh, clergymen sitting at the monastery by day and wandering with families by night, shame

Oh, disciples of impeccable devotion from the outside, but secretly cheaters, shame

Oh, physicians who accept money before giving treatment, shame

Oh, wary person, who can't see his own faults, but finds faults in others, shame

Oh, the girl whose eyes pretend to be looking at the face, but whose soul wanders around one's back, shame

Oh, masters teaching purity in the daytime, but become lax at night, shame

Oh, husbands who visit other families, but question their wives, shame

Oh, wives not hearing their husbands, and become intimate with others, shame

Oh, if these negative actions are found in me, then I am alone amid the public in shame

Oh, if these faults are found among others, no matter their position. They are also shame and shame

Ah no need for desperation. But what a pity

Oh, my poem is over.[43]

6

A DESERT THEATER

"Above a minimum level of sophistication, cultural development is bound to depend on a certain stability of life. To take a single concrete example, a proper theater cannot develop amongst wandering nomads. The Mongols were never averse to the theater, but amongst the herdsmen themselves dramatic performances never seem to have grown much beyond the size of what they themselves call the 'conversation song'… There were no costumes, no make-up and no action beyond the movement of the head and eyes."[44]

Charles Bawden

Opera was almost unheard of in early 19th-century Outer Mongolia, largely due to its distance from large metropolitan cultural centers, its scattered population and Manchu isolationist policies. Danzan Ravjaa would introduce and popularize it.

As Bawden suggests, would-be actors occasionally put on a one-man show inside a ger. These performances included epic poems, overtone singing (*khöömii*) and other songs. The usual topic of these songs was the beauty of a woman, the strength of a horse, the immensity of the landscape, the great love of a prince for a poor shepherd girl, or maybe the illicit love of a lama for a young beauty.

Some of these bards worked on a semi-professional basis, traveling across the steppes to perform their shows, as Danzan Ravjaa's father had done. Przewalski made comments on his observations of small theater and music:

> "Their songs are always plaintive and relate to their past lives and exploits. They usually sing on a caravan journey, and occasionally in the yurta, but the women's voices are not heard so often as the men's. Troubadours or wandering minstrels always secure an appreciative audience. Their musical instruments are the flute and guitar; we never saw them dance, and they are probably unskilled in the art."[45]

The epic songs (called *Baatarlag Tuul*, "heroic epic") could go on for hours or even days. They generally contained messages of prophecy, describing the future 'war of Shambhala,' and the destruction of evil. The epic songs were consistent with traditional Mongolian verse, using vowel harmony, formal parallelism and initial line alliteration. Generally, there were no prose passages, but some less able bards would resort to summarizing in prose the passages they couldn't remember in verse form.[46]

The epic songs and other verse forms were usually sung to the accompaniment of stringed instruments such as the violin, fiddle or zither. The Mongol fiddle is called *morin huur* (horsehead fiddle), named after its use of horsehair strings and unique carving (the upper portion is shaped like a horse head). The Scottish missionary James Gilmour called the Mongol fiddle "rude and primitive," but said its sound was "soft and low and pleasing in the extreme."

Gilmour describes in his book a song about a young girl, sung to him by a lama with the accompaniment of a fiddle.

"The burden of the song was the praises of the maiden named Pingling, and the words are supposed to proceed from the mouth of a disappointed suitor who is stricken with grief, when the girl finally mounts her horse and rides off in a procession to be the wife of a more fortunate rival.

The plan of the song is truly Mongolian. The various birds singing on the temple roof, twittering on the plain, and floating on the lakes, are each asked in turn, and in separate verses, if they have seen the marriage procession of the dear, the beautiful, the friendly Pingling pass along. Even the rainbow, the five-colored and nine-colored rainbow is interrogated. The procession itself is described in a series of verses, the burden and refrain of each of which is that the little Pingling is conspicuous as she rides along solitary in the center. The song also enlarges on her beauties and graces. Her skin is like cotton or snow, her breath is like musk, even her perspiration is minutely characterized in a manner which to Mongols may be eulogistic, but which would seem ridiculous to foreign ears.

It was a little difficult to start the singers in this song, but it was more difficult to stop them. Different versions seem to have different numbers of verses, and it was not till a long list of them had been slowly gone through, that an opportunity could be found to terminate the performance by praising its merits." [47]

While such performances were staged inside the ger, outdoor theater was limited. Chinese colonization in the 18th century meant the development of theater groups in the settlements of Khovd, Uliastai and Huree, but these were geared to Manchu and Chinese audiences and probably were not introduced to the greater Mongol public. There was, however, a theater production in western Mongolia called the "History of Daughter Manubari."

Rather than sitting through the Chinese-inspired productions, most Mongols preferred to watch religious dance performances called *tsam* (sometimes *cham*), which Ravjaa studied in Alasha and Chahar, and sporadically offered for the patrons of his own temples.

Tsam dance may have developed first in India, but its real origins were in pre-Buddhist Tibet, during the time when the animistic religion Bön was practiced. The priest or shaman, dressed in an elaborate costume and dancing to the beat of a drum, would embody animals or spirits while in his trance. Over time, the shamans' dance evolved into an actual form of entertainment, with the audience expecting both a religious experience and theatrical enjoyment. Thus, one aspect of dramatic theater in Central Asia was formed.

The Duinkhor quarter of Khamaryn Khiid was built specifically as a 'Tsam Theater.' It was later expanded to include more diverse forms of theater. Ravjaa assembled a skilled orchestra to accompany the tsam dances. There were no less than 24 instruments divided into four classes: wind, percussion, stringed and rattle. [48]

Part of the Shamanic ceremony included sacrificial offerings.

These, however, became unfashionable when Tibet adopted Buddhism after the 8th century. Padmasambhava, an Indian Tantric teacher, was the first to substitute the Bön characters with Buddhist ones; the bloody sacrifices were replaced with symbolic gestures (like the tearing apart of a manikin instead of a living creature). This agreed with Buddhist monks who found the sacrifice of animals abhorrent. As the centuries passed, storylines were developed, characters added and plots refined. Each region adapted the dance to reflect its own myths and beliefs but it was the larger monasteries of Tibet that standardized the dance into the tsam that we recognize today.

Typically the dance is held in the main courtyard of the monastery, on a stage called the *tsam-ra*. After the nobility and common people have taken their seats, the musicians begin to play and the first dancers appear on stage wearing wide-brimmed black hats topped with replicated human skulls. This costume is believed to represent the clothing worn by Palgye Dorje, the Tibetan monk who assassinated the fanatic anti-Buddhist King Langdarma, in the 9th century. Tibetans and Mongols would have been familiar with the plot for this story.

The story begins by describing the despotic rule of King Langdarma. A truly wicked man, he has spent his ruling life purging his people, his opponents and the monasteries of his kingdom. In response, the heroic Palgye Dorje devises a plot to topple the king. First he blackens his white horse with coal dust, then slips a bow and arrow into his long coat sleeves, and finally rides into Lhasa disguised as a Bön magician. Palgye Dorje gains an audience with the king and begins a special dance, watched by the king and his noblemen. The king becomes entranced and is drawn near, giving the monk an opportunity to shoot him with the poison-tipped arrow. The king perishes and the monk slips unnoticed out of the city. After changing back into his monks' robes, he crosses the river. It is now that the audience sees Palgye Dorje's craftiness – as his horse wades through the waters the coal dust is washed away and the horse becomes white once again. When the king's cavalry catches up with the disguised Palgye Dorje, they ask, "Have you seen a magician riding a black pony?" The monk points them in the wrong direction, makes his escape and Buddhism is saved.

The tsam dance was a common feature for Danzan Ravjaa's troupe. Danzan Ravjaa himself made occasional appearances in his own tsam performances; in 1830 Ravjaa performed in a tsam developed by the third Panchen Lama (1737-1780), which focused on the war of Shambhala and destruction of the unfaithful.

Besides tsam, Ravjaa also had his performers re-enact a stage drama of the story of Palgye Dorje and King Langdarma. Interviews conducted in 1960 by the researcher Damdinsuren show that this drama was also directed by the seventh Noyon Hutagt in the early 20th century (although some of the names had been changed).

"The actor playing the role of Langdarma killed many monks with his sword," said Yondon, one of the men interviewed by Damdinsuren. "Palgye Dorje then shot the king with his arrow and Langdarma fell over. When Palgye Dorje crossed the river his horse changed color."[49]

Ghoulish characters follow the first tsam dancers, each with terrifying, demonic masks and skull necklaces. The cast includes deformed animals, evil spirits, skeletons, Indian yogis and the Chokyi Gyalpo, a bull-headed religious king who slays the Lord of the Dead. This creature performs the ritual sacrifice by dismembering a corpse and scattering the limbs. Because these scenes are meant to instill fear, some comic moments are added to ease the audience's mind. In Mongolia, an old man with a long white beard played the comic role. The old man, named Tserendug, had been part of the pantheon of shamanic gods, a symbol of fertility for both people and livestock, and was brought into the Buddhist realm by lamas who recognized his popularity.

The tsam dance, which can last up to three days, is designed to crush evil spirits before the New Year begins. By the end of the performance, the protectors have subdued all the enemies of Buddhism and have therefore eliminated the fear of demons. Tsam dances were fairly consistent in Mongolia and Tibet, but Danzan Ravjaa toyed with the dance – altering its rules and strict conformity. First he de-emphasized the importance of Tserendug and increased the importance of female characters; actually making the old man subservient to his female protector-deity. In one scene, the female protector orders Tserendug to milk a cow. However, because of his poor eyesight he mistakenly milks an elephant. His reaction upon realizing this was a humiliating moment for Tserendug and comic relief for Ravjaa's audience.

Ravjaa also recognized the value of the human face. While masks were still used for some performances, Ravjaa had some of his actors play their parts without a mask, reasoning that their facial expressions could be just as emphatic as their dance movements. According to one legendary tale, a certain dancer named Barmasi sat backstage, fraught at having misplaced his mask. Thinking the angered expression on his face even more shocking than the mask itself, Ravjaa tied a *ganlin* (bone trumpet) into his hair and pushed him on stage to frighten the audience with his maniacal appearance.

"Playing the tsam without a mask became the fundamental tool for Mongolian theater," explains museum curator D. Bold, himself a former actor. "Facial expressions became important and this shifted stage entertainment away from dance to real acting."[50]

* * *

There were other performing arts that certainly had great influence on Ravjaa. One must have been the singing play in which two minstrels would perform a duet, exchanging verses to provide some moral for the audience. The following example, called *Galuu Hun Khoër*, written by Ravjaa, is a dialogue between a man and a goose. Together they discuss obligation and responsibility. The use of the bird shows the migrating or transitory nature of affections. The man, who tries to explain the impossibility of avoiding one's obligation, begins the conversation:

> Goose you came from the south
> Goose you spend your summer in the high Khangai
> Goose you sing on the wide water
> Will you stay here forever?

And the bird responds:

> Even when there were no clouds there was rain
> And even if no one lit anything there was smoke
> And when one looked up there were rocks
> And what one did oneself was an obligation

The man responds:

> Your rain without clouds is called hail
> Your smoke without lightning is called fog
> The rocks that you saw are called ice
> And what you did yourself is called karma

The bird comments:

    Person who works for the government

    Person who has experienced peace and happiness

    Person who has unbeatable skill

    Are you staying here long?

Then the man answers:

    I received things that I gave away before

    I became blind though I used to see

    I felt cold in the winter

    I became poor having property

    Previous good karma is returning things I gave away

    Seeing death, but not knowing it, is being blind

    Winter months are old age

    No property is the next life's soul

The goose now asks:

    How to protect from the rain without clouds?

    How to dispel the fog that wasn't generated?

    With what can the rock be destroyed?

    How to fulfill my duty?

The man says:

    Feathers can protect from the rain without clouds

    By flight, fog without generation can be avoided

    I would fly to the warm land from the ice that I have seen

    I will make my karma lighter by experiencing results of karma

By the story of this goose and man
I have set a wonderful example
For ignorant people it is a joke
For a lonely person it is entertainment[51]

The duet, performed on stage before an audience, advanced beyond the normal theater-yurt performance but it was still a far cry from modern drama. Moving closer in this direction was the Buddhist morality play called *ace lhamo.* A 15th-century Tibetan bridge builder and holy man named Thang Tong Gyalpo is credited with developing this type of theater acting – having taken the tsam dance and given it dialogue.

According to the story, a Tibetan work crew came to Thang Tong Gyalpo seeking advice. They complained that the bridge they were building by day was being disassembled by demons during the night. In order to distract the demons, he advised them to stage a play each evening. In this manner, they completed their bridge. Their play was the first ace lhamo performance.

The ace lhamo can be based on legendary or historical characters and the plots are borrowed from folktales and Buddhist canonical literature. The theatrical aspects were borrowed from India and actors are usually decked out in elaborate costumes and masks. Masks that portray animals cover the entire head while witches, devils, demons and evil foreigners wear a three-dimensional face mask. Female characters wear a flat teardrop shaped mask and the male heroes wear no mask at all. The script dialogue is stylized and is done in a singsong voice called *namtar.*

The performances, which can last a day or more, are played by a troupe that can include both monks and laypeople. At one time these troupes traveled to different temples and monasteries, bringing all their props and costumes with them. It was not only an effective way to spread Buddhist messages but also a means of employment and fund-raising. Danzan Ravjaa also set up a sort of traveling carnival called *Amaagiin Gandoi Erkh* to worship the deity Yanchin. His dancers (usually female) would visit local families, invite them to the festivities and then introduce them to his spiritual messages, while at the same time gathering up donations and gifts.

While the ace lhamo typically shows how Buddhism can defeat evil and bring happiness to the pious, some plays, including *Dalog Nangsa*, are more secular. This play describes a woman who had seen the world after death – *dalog* means 'to return from beyond' – and is applied to people who have traveled to hell. This idea stems from Tibet's Shamanic roots when souls journeyed between the worlds. According to the play, a virtuous woman called Nangsa is wrongly accused of adultery and is beaten to death by a vengeful sister-in-law. Nangsa must then face Shinje (the Lord of Death). This Erlig-type figure interrogates and then acquits her when he feels she has been unjustly murdered. Shinje allows Nangsa to return to life, but once home she is again mistreated by her friends and relatives. Escaping their cruel punishment she joins a nunnery. In the end, Nangsa flies from the roof of the convent and disappears into a rainbow.

In similar, non-secular fashion, there is the popular Mongolian story *Journey To Hell* about a noblewoman named Choidshid. While fighting a terrible sickness she dreams about her descent to the underworld where she confronts Erlig. It is decided that Choidshid is not ready to die and she is ordered back to life. But before returning to the upper world Choidshid witnesses the long

lines of people from all classes awaiting judgment. The good and
bad deeds of each are read aloud and the dead are condemned to
the appropriate hell. When she has returned to earth, she tells of
her experience and persuades her followers to lead a virtuous life
or be subjected to eternal punishment after death. It was this short
play, and others like it, which Ravjaa used as a vignette between his
main theater performances.[52]

*   *   *

Elements of tsam, morality plays and song duets can be found in
Danzan Ravjaa's most famous play, *Saran Khökhöö Namtar (The
Life Story of the Moon Cuckoo)*. He wrote the libretto in 1827-
1828 (some sources say 1830-1831) in the quiet isolation of Khar
Uul (Black Mountains), not far from Khamaryn Khiid. The story
is based on a novel written in 1737 by a Tibetan writer known
as Madi (whose given name was Dagfu Luvson Dambi Jaltsen).
A 71-year-old Inner Mongolian monk, Dai Guosh Vangindara
Shasna Varda (otherwise known as Agvanlampil), translated the
play into Mongolian in 1770. Danzan Ravjaa was probably first
exposed to *Saran Khökhöö* in the monasteries of Alasha. Despite
being of Tibetan origin, Ravjaa's nine-act version was adapted
for a Mongolian audience, including Mongolian games, sports,
traditions and social life, covering a 20-year period of time in the
19th century. *Saran Khökhöö* was usually shown in one day, but
there were other versions that could take one week, two weeks or
a 12-volume version that lasted an entire month (June 15 until
July 15). The longer versions included three separate performances
based on textual biographies of Milarepa, Atisha and the historical
Buddha. The story of Palgye Dorje and King Langdarma was also
added, leading many viewers into the mistaken belief that King

Langdarma was actually part of the *Saran Khökhöö Namtar*.

Putting on a full theatrical performance in 19th-century Mongolia was no easy task. There were no drama groups, no playhouses, no costumes, nor any history of organized theater at all. Working from scratch, Ravjaa wrote scripts, choreographed music, trained actors and built stages. *Saran Khökhöö* required over 200 musicians, actors and assistants whom Ravjaa drew from all walks of life – young, old, rich, poor, lamas and lay people.

One difference between this opera and the Tibetan ace lhamo was that Danzan Ravjaa's characters usually did not wear masks. They used make-up, a technique probably borrowed from Chinese opera. Aristocrats and bureaucrats (when they performed in Ravjaa's plays) were allowed to wear masks to disguise their identity – there was concern that the unsophisticated audience would mock a wealthy aristocrat for playing the role of a poor person. In some cases, Ravjaa may have used animal masks to differentiate good and bad characters: monkey, tiger, donkey, pig and cow heads were villains while cuckoo, human and horse heads were heroes.

Danzan Ravjaa and his disciples rehearsed the opera in the Khar Uul Mountains and Alasha. Preparations complete, the first shows were performed in the urban centers of Inner Mongolia. Monies raised from their performances were used to fund his monasteries in Outer Mongolia. Monastery courtyards served as the main venues, the same stages used by the Tibetan tsam performers. In Outer Mongolia, Ravjaa went one step further and built three special-purpose theaters.

The first theater was a simple tent structure pitched at the foot of a mountain in the Khar Uul range. The second theater was constructed in Süm Khökh Burd in Dundgobi, set upon the ruins of an old temple. The original construction here dated from the 10th century. Later, a small nobleman's home was erected in the 17th century. Danzan Ravjaa's stage was built over the fallen masonry.

The largest theater was adjacent to Khamaryn Khiid. The impressive structure was commissioned in 1832, shortly after Ravjaa made his epic journey to Agui Süm and pilgrimage to Kumbun Monastery (Ta'er Si) in Amdo. The project took two full years to complete, during which time Ravjaa sent his actors (*hurigchid*) to Alasha for training.

The three-story building was positioned close to the monastery complex; the stone foundations are still visible in the ground. The main action was on the first platform, which featured a trap door, stage exits on both sides and well-placed mirrors that could be used for exchanging signals. Off to the sides were the dressing rooms and make-up rooms. Comic intermissions were staged on the second tier. Sometimes two scenes were shown simultaneously, the first floor representing the earth and the second floor, the sky or heaven. This was useful because many Buddhist dramas had alternating scenes between heaven and earth, heaven and hell or earth and hell. Gombo, a former resident lama at Khamaryn Khiid, tells how the multi-level stage was also used to show class distinction: "The lords feasted on the top floor while the slaves spoke of all things from the lower floor. Some slaves said their master was a good man like the Buddha while others said their master was evil-minded like the Devil."[53]

A directors' box was located on the third floor. Several observers, including Danzan Ravjaa, could sit here and oversee the opera below. Signals and directions could be given using mirrors. One of his assistants held a short wooden staff with pieces of silk and cloth tied to one end; this device was used to flog actors who made mistakes (more humiliating than it was physically painful).

The 64-member orchestra – filled with string, wind and percussion instruments – sat hidden behind the main stage. Towards the back, and on each side, were rooms for the 30-odd crew members who organized costumes and stage design.

The historian Dogmid wrote, "The acoustics were so good that men seated on their camels in the back row could hear the actors perfectly."[54] Baatar, a senior lama at Khamaryn Khiid, describes a sort of 'magical wind' that could carry the actor's voices out to the audience, but prevented the spectator's chatter from reaching the stage. A more reasonable explanation is that the architects wisely positioned the building so the prevailing winds swept towards the audience, carrying voices and music with it.

Whole teams were involved in pre-production costume design, props and make-up. Others were assigned as music and acting instructors. Costumes for the opera were elaborate and heavy – large silk gowns with oversized sleeves and cuffs, weighed down by semi-precious stones and shiny metallic objects. Some examples of these costumes are on display at the Danzan Ravjaa museum, including the small, knee-high boots worn by the young actor who played the part of the cuckoo. Yellow in color, they feature upturned toes of the traditional Mongol boot with a cuckoo's head at the tip, as well as an embroidered image of the cuckoo bird at the top, covering the calf. Face make-up was produced in Mongolia from clarified yak butter, grease and paint made from crushed stones. The different colors symbolized emotion; red, for example, represented courage while white was indicative of cunning.

Special effects were another main feature of the theater at Khamaryn Khiid. Ravjaa was renowned for mystifying his audience with simulated weather. First came the roll of thunder using drums made with stretched leather skins, then the crack of lighting with the help of Chinese firecrackers. The backstage doors were opened to allow in a funnel of wind. Then came the pitter-patter of rain when rice or seeds were dropped from the second floor and onto the stage.

As mentioned earlier, the monk Yondon had provided a verbal account of the theatrics that he saw directed by the Seventh Noyon Hutagt. Yondon recalled seeing the curious effect of Palgye Dorje's horse change color after crossing the river in the tsam dance. Yondon also remembered dramatic battle scenes. Lasting two or three days, these war epics included the use of cavalry. Twenty or thirty horsemen could 'ride' across the stage on mock horses behind a curtain that hid their legs but revealed the horses' head and rear. The fighting, he said, included swords dipped in red paint that was splattered about like so much blood.[55]

Saran Khökhöö itself is extraordinarily complex, made more so by numerous tangent scenes that break off to describe social life and religion in Mongolia. It has long received mixed reviews, as its earliest critics, the Manchus, were disturbed with what they felt was an anti-imperialistic attempt to undermine their power. A disapproving Manchurian regent once ordered Ravjaa's theater burnt to the ground, but was narrowly dissuaded by the monks of Khamaryn Khiid. On the other side of the spectrum, researcher Walther Heissig, who found part of the story in Beijing, called *Saran Khökhöö* "an astonishingly compact and thrilling story, if one overlooks the didactic passages."[56]

Heissig was, perhaps, so aroused because *Saran Khökhöö* was quite unlike the typical 18th-century Asian tale. This was an era when high-minded Buddhist stories were fashionable, spurred by the hierarchy's long-lasting fight to crush superstition and paganism. *Saran Khökhöö*, especially the Mongolian version, read like a real-life drama and was uniquely adventurous, and, although it carried Buddhist morals, its focus and uniqueness was on humanity.

The play looks into social conflicts, the distinction between good and evil, wisdom and dullness, the rich and poor. It examines how these different values interact to form the world in which Danzan Ravjaa lived. The major theme shows how blackmail and sin are unscrupulously used for ruling class power grabs, but the story does not outwardly seek to sway the opinion of the audience. Rather, it presents itself in a way that allows the public to judge the characters for themselves. It was this aspect that was uniquely Ravjaa, and uniquely Mongolian.

* * *

The story begins with a description of King Mashuka, whose wife gives birth to a beautiful girl, on whose cheek is the vague outline of a chrysanthemum and whose whole body bears the scent of this flower. A lama announces that the child is a special reincarnation and her father bestows upon her a religious name, Madmakhya. King Odibisha, who rules a neighboring kingdom, visits this marvelous child and word spreads of her beauty. Soon all the kings come to Mashuka's palace and a sacrificial ritual is held to honor the exalted child.

Years later, Madmakhya is a grown woman and indeed very beautiful. Countless princes and kings arrive at the palace to ask for her hand in marriage, but Mashuka cannot decide among them. So he instructs the courtiers to dress in their finest clothes and Madmakhya will decide for herself by tossing one of them a flower rosary. When they line up, the court believes she will send her rosary towards one of two very powerful and wealthy kings. Instead she throws it to an unknown prince in a *tsagaan del* (white robe with a silk sash) named Guleranz. This attire brought him the nickname 'Tsagaan Del.' When her father asks why she had thrown it to this prince of mediocre wealth, she answers that money and looks are not her priority. Knowledge is more important and she is confident Guleranz is the right man to take as her husband.

Together the wise king and queen live and rule in Varnasi, India. They are a popular and well-respected royal couple, and they enjoy all of life's pleasures, with the exception of a child. So they pray to their protector deities, and ten months later Madmakhya gives birth to a beautiful boy who they name Nomun-Bayasgalant.

Other important characters introduced here are the two Brahmins named Garma-Öd and Suzaa. Add to the list Guleranz's trusted Minister Yamshe, a two-faced character who appears kindly but is actually cold-hearted and wicked.

Yamshe has a son named Laganaa and very much wants his child to follow in his footsteps. He suggests to Guleranz that Laganaa befriend Nomun-Bayasgalant so they can start a relationship of prince and servant. This intrigue is told as follows in the script:

> "The high minister thought, aye! I have been a friend with King Guleranz since our youth, thus he loves me very much. Even today though I am old I have much power over him. If my son does not befriend Nomun-Bayasgalant from an early age he will never reach a high status. Even today I have the power to run the country and as long as I am alive I must take the opportunity to assist my son. Thus the king's little one must give the might to that boy. He must take him to be the bearer of honors and when he

takes my son as a friend, this one (my boy) will always get land in great style."[57]

Guleranz says he will take the matter up with his wife. But Yamshe, who fears Madmakhya, tells Guleranz "*Real* kings do not consult with their wives." Somehow Madmakhya learns of Yamshe's plot and she is immediately against the friendship. She instinctively does not trust the minister but pride forces Guleranz to reject her demands that Yamshe be dismissed. "*Real* kings do not listen to their wives," he tells her.

Three wise men also appear in the story and are likewise against the friendship of Laganaa and Nomun-Bayasgalant. They go to the king's chamber to warn Guleranz, but are betrayed by spies deployed by Yamshe. The minister conjures up a story that the wise men plotted to assassinate the king and manages to have them banished from Varnasi. Before expulsion they announce that "Life is now hard but the times to come will be more difficult." In this way, Yamshe is able to secure the friendship between Nomun-Bayasgalant and Laganaa.

The two boys study and play together, and for some time life in Varnasi is peaceful. One day Nomun-Bayasgalant hears about a powerful Brahmin named Taruba, and he asks Laganaa to visit this wise man. Laganaa agrees and during the meeting it is revealed that this Brahmin has the power to animate dead bodies. Laganaa reports his discovery to Nomun-Bayasgalant, and the two go together to the Brahmin to learn how to animate dead creatures. Soon they are both skilled in this art.

As Nomun-Bayasgalant grows up he considers that he should leave the palace, shed his rich silk clothing and become a monk. This is a typical aspect of Buddhist stories, which reflects

Siddhartha's intention to do the same. Guleranz objects on the grounds that the prince should be married, have children and keep the royal line intact. He forbids Nomun-Bayasgalant from going into the monastic life and marries him to a beautiful, wise and kind-hearted woman from middle India named Sersnaa.[58] Being a pragmatic woman she does not object to her husband's interest in Buddhism. Rather, she suggests that they study the faith together.

Sersnaa and Nomun-Bayasgalant are very fond of each other, and their relationship disgusts the second of his five wives. The second is an evil and jealous character called Sersadanii.[59] In order to destroy this relationship and fulfill her dreams of becoming the primary queen, Sersadanii befriends Laganaa.

At first the young minister resists the plans of this lovely temptress. He says it would be quite impossible for him to betray Nomun-Bayasgalant, as they have been friends since childhood. But after much persuasion he eventually concedes to her wishes and agrees to think of some plot by which he can overthrow the prince.

One day Laganaa suggests to Nomun-Bayasgalant that ministers of the court visit a lovely garden on the outskirts of Varnasi, to which the prince agrees. Before leaving, Laganaa takes two dead cuckoo birds with him. After seeing the garden, Laganaa suggests to the prince that they walk to a beautiful wide river which is not far away. Upon reaching the riverbank, Laganaa says that across the river is a secret forest that they should explore. The prince suggests that they borrow a boat from his father and paddle across the river. The cunning Laganaa says Guleranz would not give permission to take a boat, but he has another idea. The young minister reveals the two dead cuckoos and suggests they animate them and fly across the river to secretly explore the forest.

Overcome by curiosity, Nomun-Bayasgalant agrees to the plan and the two friends leave their human forms and enter the cuckoos' bodies. They fly over the river and into the forest, and are immediately overwhelmed by its tempting fruit and rare flowers. But while Nomun-Bayasgalant is lost in this wonderland and enjoying the singing birds, the underhanded Laganaa flies back across the river to the bank where the inanimate bodies still lie. He leaves the cuckoo body and takes the flesh of Nomun-Bayasgalant. Then he throws the cuckoo corpse and his own inanimate body into the river.

Laganaa, now with the prince's body, returns to the palace entourage, crying that his "dear friend Laganaa" has fallen into the river and drowned. All the courtiers lament this tragic incident and mourn for "dead" Laganaa.

Everyone returns to the palace to mourn the loss. However, in the coming days Sersnaa, the principal wife, begins to have doubts about the death of Laganaa. Her husband still looks like Nomun-Bayasgalant but is now a changed man, having no interest in Buddhism or prayer. She soon finds the prince repulsive and is even more disgusted when he begins giving special attention to the wicked concubine Sersadanii. It isn't long before the beautiful and kind Sersnaa is banished from the palace. She has no choice but to live an ordinary life as a penniless peasant outside the castle walls.

Meanwhile, the real Nomun-Bayasgalant is still in the glen across the river, fluttering about in his cuckoo body. He is worried for his feathered friend Laganaa who has gone missing, when the Buddha appears before him and explains what has happened. The sympathetic Buddha also turns into a cuckoo to keep the saddened prince company and tells Nomun-Bayasgalant that his fate is to remain in the forest with the other animals.

Hence the sad prince remains in his feathered form and lives amongst the birds, teaching them Buddhism and magic. Nineteenth-century Mongolian audiences would certainly be able to connect this with the legend of the Buddha preaching to the birds (which occurs in some of the "Jataka Tales" of his previous lives). They may also have associated the bird with Danzan Ravjaa, who was himself an outcast of Manchu authority, preaching his good words to those with an ear to listen.

Back at the palace, servants and attendants are concerned over the dire state of affairs among the royal family members. 'Nomun-Bayasgalant' becomes very cruel – punishing his subjects without cause, confiscating their property and greedily reveling in his wealth. He no longer helps beggars, and instead suppresses Buddhism and education. Beauty, it appears, is only 'skin deep' and the court can no longer trust their prince. The lines of one villager:

> "We were mistaken in our thoughts that we lived under an educated king and that our happiness was never-ending. Now we have no time for happiness. This month is worse than the previous month and this year is worse than the past year. These days a man with beautiful daughters is more important than the clever man. And drunken youths are better than old honest clerks. Killing and robbery is more common than religious activities and the good system of the old times is destroyed."[60]

Sersnaa is the first to recognize that this evil prince cannot be her husband. She writes a letter describing her suspicions, leaves it on the palace door, and flees to her homeland. While traveling home, she meets the three banished wise men who had faithfully served Guleranz. They understand the problem in their kingdom and are determined to return home and restore order. After their long journey the wise men ride around the village outside the palace and announce that Nomun-Bayasgalant is not really who he appears to be. Realizing that the scheme is unwinding, Laganaa's father Yamshe commits suicide, and his mother dies of grief. Laganaa, still in the form of Nomun-Bayasgalant, flees the palace and is never seen again.

Tragically, the blue-throated cuckoo-prince can do nothing more than perch on the windowsill of his castle. According to what the Buddha in the forest had predicted, a famous lama who preaches long-winded Buddhist sermons meets the cuckoo and explains how all the preceding events were connected to the spiritual world. For example, the bad karma associated with Nomun-Bayasgalant and Laganaa is connected to a past life when they had been neighboring kings who had warred with each other.

The cuckoo eventually dies of a broken heart and Nomun-Bayasgalant is found in the bird's body. In the end, he is buried underneath an evergreen tree while flowers rain down from the sky. For years to come the tree is worshiped by the people of Varnasi.[61]

*   *   *

There are two primary elements at work in this opera. The first is Ravjaa's use of the play to show important elements of Buddhist thought and philosophy. *Saran Khökhöö* showed people how to live righteous lives according to the Buddha's teachings and if these teachings were ignored they could expect karmic retribution. In the case of Laganaa and Nomun-Bayasgalant, bad karma from a previous lifetime taught them both painful lessons. Tantric ideas also occur throughout, notably with the recognition of feminine knowledge as an important source of power, as well as secret spells, such as the ability of the two boys to animate the dead.

The second important element of the opera is Ravjaa's surreptitious attempts at political satire. As a social critic, the director designed the play so that it devalued the petty aristocracy. Greedy noblemen, oppressive Manchurian officials and illegitimate rule are displayed through Yamshe's and Sersadanii's intense desire for power. The two ultimately ruin the kingdom with their personal ambitions. Danzan Ravjaa shows that this is not a historical play but rather a story told about the present. In the original libretto we can find such phrases like, "When bad times come," which Ravjaa changed to read, "In these bad times," showing a desire to criticize contemporary society. The play becomes even more personal when it becomes clear that the director is using characters to display his own emotions. Ravjaa, for example, was surely expressing his own thoughts about contemporary society when King Mashuka said:

> Most of the people look at the colors, not at the quality
> Sick for beauty, not for kindness
> Look for benefit, not for good behavior
> People want fame rather than good thoughts
> They don't have good conduct, just false words
> So it is a bad time[62]

Mongolian Professor Tsagaan summed up this expressive mood when she wrote, "Even though he is a representative of the highest class, he can still criticize his contemporaries. He said if the government acts badly then ordinary people will suffer. The drama is clear proof that he was progressive and loved his country and people. He expressed all his critical ideas through this drama."[63]

The play accomplished more than the teaching of lessons; it also promoted Mongolian culture in the face of encroaching Chinese influence. Ravjaa, fearing that the Mongols would be sinocized by their southern neighbors, did justice to Mongolian social life and leisure activities. He emphasized the importance of classical Mongolian sporting events like horse racing, archery, and wrestling. He also incorporated ancient customs: for example, when Prince Nomun-Bayasgalant is born, his parents give a piece of white felt to a fortune-teller. The seer was able to look into this felt and see Nomun-Bayasgalant's future. He fearfully describes a tortured life of sadness and heartache. For centuries, Mongolian fortune-tellers have used the same method for predicting the future of newborn babies.

The flowery and descriptive language Ravjaa uses in the play is common in Mongolian classic literature. The following extract, a dialogue between the dying King Mashuka and his daughter Madmakhya, exemplifies the language used:

> Oh, daughter you listen!
> Leaves are not always on trees
> Children are not always together with their parents
> The dragon's call will become empty though its roar is loud
> The world's triumph will pass away though its glory is great
> Colorful rainbows will disappear though they are beautiful

Lovely young bodies will grow old though they are now young

Thousands of millions of dreams are empty when you wake up

Every act of this naïve life is false at the time of death

Night comes if the sun sets

Death comes when age ends

Death – a strong winged bird can't escape from it

There is no shelter from death

There is no wise word to fight with death

There is no trick for death

You can't do anything to delay death

You can't die with your friend

Wealth cannot be sacrificed to save you

You can't be against death because of haughty power

Does the wind blow in any direction?

Is there any date with death?

If death comes nothing can help except the Dharma

Don't be worried about being separated from your old father

Create a prayer called 'Büd Erdene' when you go to the place you have never been

If you have something to ask me then ask now[64]

Such elegant and descriptive prose is indicative of why so much time was needed to stage the performance. In the longer versions, dozens of other characters are introduced, although they had little to do with the main plot. They serve as side acts for additional commentary on Mongolian life and philosophy. One such character was the one-eyed, one-toothed, one-breasted, good woman of the mountain, who acted as a sort of creator-ogress, and was used to show the audience female strength. A mask of this character can be found today in the Danzan Ravjaa Museum. Tibetan scholars may recognize this character as Tsechigma (Sanskrit: Ekajati) who, according to Tibetan legend, fought Padmasambhava and was subdued. She also functions as one of the three principal protectors of Dzogchen, the Nyingma's highest teaching order.

*   *   *

Theatergoers were probably pleased to see that Danzan Ravjaa included a number of humorous and insightful vignettes to the opera. These were played during intermissions to lighten up an otherwise heavy plot and provide further lessons in morality and mockery of Manchu authority. One popular intermission was a comic ballet called 'How Punishment Was Given to Five Witches.' In this story, a heavenly prince descends to Khamaryn Khiid and is welcomed by its people. Suddenly, a one-eyed, lame, Chinese hunchback appears on stage and secretly tells five witches about the lovely prince. The evil witches, lusting after the handsome young man, disguise themselves as five famous angels and are also welcomed by the people of Khamaryn Khiid. The head lama, however, is suspicious of the angels and asks the advice of Danzan Ravjaa, who makes a cameo appearance on stage.

"What is the use of a monk's studies if he cannot detect the difference between good and evil?" Danzan Ravjaa asks.

He then advises the monk to hold a great feast. In the following act, the witches appear on stage, drunk and staggering amid the other festival goers. Danzan Ravjaa quietly asks a master sculptor named Baramsi to create an image of the prince and in a very short time the work is complete. The witches see the statue and, mistaking it for the real prince, scoop it up and fly away. While in the sky they realize their folly, but they are too late; the real angels arrive at Khamaryn Khiid and carry the prince back to heaven. The vignette is much like a children's fairy tale, providing a lesson in morality and a pleasant ending.

Other vignettes included slapstick comedy routines. In one performance, the curtain opens to reveal an old man, his wife and their son sleeping in bed. Suddenly the Buddha appears in their home and the awe-struck wife falls on her knees to pray. Likewise, the father falls to pray but in the dark of night manages to plant his face squarely into his wife's rear end. At that moment their son then wakes up. Horrified to see his father in such an unceremonious position, he begs his father to pray to the Buddha. "I have, my son," the elder says. "I've prayed to the Buddha and your mother too."[65]

A third comic skit shows a butcher wearing a black del and a black hat. These costume ideas were probably borrowed from the first act of tsam. The butcher cries out at the top of his voice, "Meat! Meat for sale! Buy meat!"

An old lama soon hobbles onto the stage and asks, "How many animals have you killed?"

The butcher replies proudly, "So many that I cannot count them all."

The lama grows angry and, poking the butcher with his cane, says, "Stop killing animals! That is a sinful act! You must now be ordained as a lama to repent for your sins!" When the butcher protests, the lama gives him a string of rosary beads and instructs him how to chant. The butcher, a practical man, takes the rosary and uses it to count the number of animals he has killed. The lama, again angered, grabs his dagger, presses it against the butcher's throat and growls through clenched teeth, "Now are you going to become a lama?"

Needless to say, the cowardly butcher dons the yellow robes of a lama and begins to learn the prayers. But when the old lama leaves, the butcher cries out, "What a detestable occupation!" He tears off the yellow clothes, grabs his sack full of sheep parts and cries out, "Meat! Meat for sale!"

The scene is not only comic, but also serves a purpose in degrading hypocritical lamas. It is also a clear example of Danzan Ravjaa's ability to criticize the faith to which he was dedicated, a commendable ability in any time or culture.

"Life was difficult then because Mongolia was under the control of the Manchus," explained the researcher D. Bold. "Ravjaa was relentless in his attack on societal wrongs and the Manchus, but not directly. He was a master at concealing his humor and ideas but by the end of the performance most of the audience should feel shame. He criticized religion, the rich, the poor, the powerful, unfaithful women and charlatan monks. He had a real sense of society."

Such vignettes were carefully programmed for specific audiences. Anti-Manchu or anti-imperial references were omitted when performances were held in front of visiting Manchurian officials, who Mongols saw as a people easily offended. Likewise, *Saran Khökhöö* itself contained some degrading references to imperialist rule that were absent from the larger events staged at Khamaryn Khiid. The smaller, less advertised performances – usually those held at remote monasteries and thus not attended by Manchus or their supporters – were the venues at which Ravjaa delivered his most scathing attacks on authority.

*   *   *

Saran Khökhöö remained on stage for years after Ravjaa's death, even into the 1920s. The scripts, props and costumes were kept safe by the lamas of Khamaryn Khiid and it was the seventh Noyon Hutagt who was largely responsible for the revival of the play after a period of theatrical inactivity. He staged the play at Khamaryn Khiid and other locations, including Tsagaan Tolgoi Temple in Khanbogd sum, Dornogobi province. In 1960, the livestock-breeder Yondon, interviewed by Damdinsuren, remembered watching the play at a two-story theater that opened onto a large courtyard. Like Danzan Ravjaa, the seventh Noyon Hutagt invited people from all walks of life to perform in the play. The Buduun Mergen Van himself (the regional prince) played the role of Guleranz.

There were differences, of course, between the performances directed by the fifth and the seventh hutagts, one of which was the use by the seventh hutagt of a large prompt book set in front of the stage for use by the actors, but hidden from the audience. In 1987, an 85-year-old Gobi native named Sundi gave an interview in regards to his role as a stagehand in a 1920 performance of *Saran Khökhöö* at Tsagaan Tolgoi Temple.

"I remember that sixty people with thirty camels arrived in our village. They announced that they would perform a one-month-long drama. They erected several gers and we could hear their music and singing in the evenings, but children were not allowed there," Sundi recalled. "They built a large stage and then came to us requesting forty volunteers to act in the drama as soldiers. They gave some lessons and selected the characters. They said I was too young for acting but let me draw and close the curtains.

"The seventh Noyon Hutagt, who was the director, was a well-built man with a dark face. It seemed as if he was always drunk. He gave all the instructions and told me how to raise the curtain. When the gong was hit twice it meant to lower the curtain part way, a long gong meant to lower it all the way.

"The audience was very emotional during the performance – people were falling in front of the actors that were dressed like gods as if they were in a temple. People came from all over to see it and soon there were tents everywhere. Nice gers and a special dining tent were made for aristocrats. I remember that each day a different actor played the king, so that many people had a chance to play the role. The show went from morning to evening and had a two-hour break at midday; a trumpeter announced when the play was starting again," Sundi concluded. [66]

Saran Khökhöö, along with the rest of the Danzan Ravjaa cult, was resurrected from its grave after 1990. The theater group in Sainshand staged excerpts of the drama in 1993, shortly after they renamed their playhouse 'Saran Khökhöö Theater.' The performance was made in front of a packed audience and drew on local talent including several lamas. D. Sanjmetov, a Sainshand native who has worked at the theater since 1967, played the part of Yamshe.

"It is a wonderful libretto, especially because it was written at a time when there was no drama. The use of singing, dancing and artwork was a landmark. It offered different messages on different levels, but one of the main ideas is respect for women and humanity in general," Sanjmetov said.

Sanjmetov explains that before 1990 the local feeling towards Ravjaa was one of mistrust. Many locals considered him a drunken womanizer. But Sanjmetov explains that democracy brought with it a change in attitude.

"We didn't study Danzan Ravjaa during communism, but now we see him in the real light. He has come to be a symbol of the Gobi and I think we are all his children."

Sanjmetov said if financial conditions are met, his theater group dreams of putting on *Life Story of the Moon Cuckoo* in its original form, as a one-month epic.

Contemporary portrait of Danzan Ravjaa

Cover of *Saran Khökhöö* manuscript

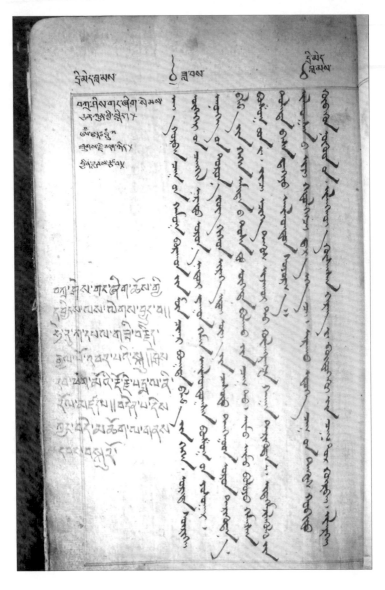

Saran Khökhöö manuscript (in Mongol and Tibetan script)

Above: Lyrics for songs and musical scores

Below: Buddhist paintings from the Danzan Ravjaa Museum

Costume worn in the play *Saran Khökhöö*

Above: Stupa at Khamaryn Khiid

Below: Baatar Lam, Enkhjargal Lam and a novice
monk at the Yolkoi caves

Above: Lama at Khamaryn Khiid

Below: Guardian family of the sacred mountain
of the Third Hutagt

Above and below: Curator Altangerel and his son Altan-Ochir
at Khamaryn Khiid

7

THE GREAT POET

"Mongolian literature is like a huge garden with beautiful smelling flowers and trees; one of the most beautiful flowers in this garden is Danzan Ravjaa's writing. When you read his works you can feel music and artwork, you will understand dance and hear the thundering of horses' hooves, you will imagine the love between a boy and girl and you will smell the sweet scent of airag."[67]

D. Tsagaan

While he was renowned for his dramatic productions, Danzan Ravjaa would have considered himself first and foremost a poet. So finely crafted was his prose that the Mongolist Walther Heissig was moved to compare its "lyrical depth and thematic breadth" to that of J.W. Goethe. Indeed Ravjaa's countrymen must have had great respect for his words – scribes diligently noted down his poetry as it spilled from his lips, whether he was sober or drunk.

Ravjaa was not merely piecing words together for the sake of creating proper or beautiful poetic works. He wrote when events moved him. His poetry contains the lessons he had learnt in his life.

It both condemns and gives praise. It is appreciative and critical. It expresses the love of his homeland, the splendor of nature, the strength of horses, the beauty of women, and the importance of integrating human life with the natural world. Deeply etched with love for life, his poetry reached out to the romantics and visionaries of his time.

Never before had a poet brought lyrics so close to the public. This accomplishment was even recognized during the latter part of the communist era, when educators began promoting Danzan Ravjaa's poetry with their own Marxist spin.

Ravjaa's poetry showed his ambiguity as a man torn between deep religious commitment and love of secular life. At one and the same time his works compare, as Heissig writes, to the Latin poetry of the Middle Ages in their drunkenness and vivacious praise of women, while at the same time showing his awareness of finality and need for ethics to propel him in the next life.

Alcohol played a significant role in his writings. He often signed at the end of his poems, "son of Dulduit, crazy drunken Ravjaa wrote this," or "the dumb drinker wrote this poem." Ironically, such statements only seem to add to his allure as a mysterious and true hutagt. Ravjaa, however, rarely condoned drinking. At times he recognized it as a sin: "Tasty, tasty – but its black spirits. If you examine it well it's one of the eight hells," he wrote in the poem 'Three Jewel Lama.'[68]

Since Ravjaa wrote while both sober and drunk, the poetry itself has a duality about it – oscillating from clear-headed teachings and observations of the world to romantic ramblings that often end with vague abruptness. Danzan Ravjaa, however, did not personally write all of his poetry. Scribes, including his principal assistants Haliut and Jamynshagvar, were on hand to write down the poems as Ravjaa dictated them. These scribes may also have assisted in editing the poetry.

Allegory and comparative phrases are common in his poetic works. "Although salt is bitter by itself, it is pleasing if part of a dish," he wrote. "Although the taste of wine is sour, it beautifies the festival."[69] His poetry is also influenced by Tibetan and Indian literature, as well as Chinese proverbs, sometimes borrowing lines from Confucius. He employed traditional folklore, mentioning in his poem 'Relieving Soul' the Pancha Tantra, the classic Indian moral story of an elephant, monkey, rabbit and bird, the four of whom climb upon each other's backs to reach a tree filled with fruit.

As a man who lived in desolate areas and often traveled across huge landscapes, it is not surprising that nature filled a prominent role in Ravjaa's writings. While admiring the world around him, speaking lovingly of summer weather and flowers in bloom, Ravjaa also understood that nature can be daunting and powerful, as described in the poem 'Full Moon of the Month.'

When we have the full moon
We can see far
For a clever person
Future events are clear

By riding my horse
I crossed the mountain
Since I am a man
I have to wade through life

And a strong eagle with rich feathers
Flies above the Khangai
Thinking about myself
I became distant from the earth

Only the sun has light
And I could see far
In the younger years of my life
I left the earth with suffering

The poor eagle fledgling
Is lost in the forest
And young ones are poor
Who are lost among the humans[70]

The deep attachment to the land coupled with the pain endured
as man "wades through life" reflects Ravjaa's dual persona as a man
in love with the world and also tortured by it. Reflecting upon his
childhood, Ravjaa recalls being "lost" amongst the human race and
leaving the suffering of the Earth, which may reflect his heartache
as a beggar boy and later entry into the protected micro-world of
the monastery. Yet never satisfied even with his privileged status,
he bemoans his distance from reality and regrets that he could not
simply fly into the world like a bird. The binary use of distance
and closeness seems to be an aspect of his Buddhist education,
which taught him that the world could be simultaneously far off
and immediate. The poem delivers a strong message that even a
man of such 'perfection' can be torn apart by troubled emotions.

When Ravjaa speaks of "leaving the Earth with suffering" he
makes a reference to the Buddhist belief in transcending the Wheel

of Life.

Buddhist ideas do not just filter into Ravjaa's poetry; they are at the root of all his poetry. 'Perfect Quality' (*Ulemchin Chanar*), for example, is one of many poems that appears outwardly unrelated to Buddhism, as it speaks mainly of the human senses. Yet from the point of view of someone practicing tantra, there is the belief that the senses in and of themselves do not impede enlightenment; in fact they are inseparable from their enlightened nature.

The poem connects one's behavior and flowers; a face with a mirror; a voice with the soft melody of a cuckoo bird; and the body with the scent of a sandal tree. The natural world, together with a passion for women and his love for Dadishura to whom it was dedicated, drives the poem forward. By the end of the poem the reader feels that Ravjaa's soul is still unsatisfied but that this will one day change. Ravjaa, however, seems content to simply acknowledge the nature of his self, that he can become even happier even before all his desires have been conquered.

> Full of immense quality
> Your beautiful face
> Just like a clear mirror
> When I see it, my perfect body[71]
> Indeed captures my soul
>
> The one who softens my hard heart
> Your soft polite words
> Just like melodies of a cuckoo bird
> When we talk awhile, your words
> So encourage me
> My sweet-mannered one

Your elegant body brings an exquisite scent
The moment I meet you
Just like the sweet scent of sandalwood
Originally created together,
It deeply moves my soul

Your joyful behavior
Just like the taste of honey
Which boils over from the lotus heart
Content with being unsatisfied
Increases the joy

In this human life
Let's float and be happy
On the ocean of bottomless happiness
Like attributes of the God of Love
After fulfilling all desires[72]

* * *

Ravjaa's later works are increasingly politicized, often filled with scathing and negative commentary about people in power. His passion does not wane over time but was diverted from those early love songs to more critical and social issues.

This was a break from the normal restrictions of Mongolian poetry. 'Shame and Shame,' which we saw in the previous chapter, was not merely acclaimed for its powerful language and critical thought. It was also viewed as an example of proper Mongolian poetry, which maintains strict rules and structure.

Ideally in Mongolian poetry, each four-line stanza should start with the same letter, and each line should end with the same word. The first letter and last word are referred to as the "head and tail." Composing such poetry is no easy feat and Ravjaa often reminded his readers of this. At the end of one 27-line poem using words that began with 'E' he wrote: "The son of Dulduit sang this by combining e-words." In another poem he reminds the reader, "rhyming with the letter U was done by the shorn Ravjaa."

This sort of 'rhyming' with the use of shared letters is virtually unknown in English literature.

'Shame and Shame' is a poetic form of Ravjaa's many *surgaal* (teachings, lessons). The surgaals, aimed squarely at his disciples, can be likened to those written by the eastern Mongol prince To-Van (mentioned in chapter five), although Ravjaa's tended to include more religious-minded material. Take for example this surgaal which criticizes disrespectful monks.

When (students) are in front of their teacher's face,
They close their eyes and pray
When (students) don't see their teacher's face,
They lie in their own thoughts.

Students promise to follow their teacher's order,
But these are deceptions.
They protect belongings of their friends,
But their teacher's belongings are of no concern.

They hide their friend's secrets
Close to their heart.
They will reveal the kind words
Of their teacher like thunder.

Students would not step on their teacher's sitting mat
When they are nearby.
When teachers leave,
The students disregard their belongings.

When students feel pleasant
They believe their own power has caused this.
When bad things occur
The students blame their teachers.[73]

Not all of Ravjaa's teachings were so contentious. He also wrote several proverbs that are still spoken today. For couples he advised the following: "If you have a fine lover, please keep a watch on your thoughts. If you have a bad lover, please test your urge to travel far."[74] Similarly, some of these teachings were put into lyrical form. Ravjaa uses the following poem to counsel his followers to appreciate life and recognize rewards.

Arise early in the morning
Look at the high sky
It will give you space
To your mind

Have an idea in the evening
Have a look at the sky with stars
And the beautiful world will love
You forever

When the sun rises
Be impressed and look at it

This shining ball will be there in the heaven
Blessing you by prosperity

Clever man wherever you go
Look at the staggering tops of mountains
This ever-precious nature
Will bless you

Whoever you meet
Look at him with a smile of friendly politeness
And then you will
Live with happiness and health for a long time

Ravjaa's choice of words in this and his other poems was important in his role as an educator. He had a great command of the Mongol language, providing truth and wisdom that could be understood by his largely uneducated audience. Still, the richness of his vocabulary was striking in the poetic sense. Tsagaan praised his writing skills and comments with the following on Ravjaa's teachings.

"Danzan Ravjaa's lessons played a considerable role in the moral education of the people. Ravjaa did not draw himself away from the life of the people. He was a contemplative person, he lived amongst the commoners and he was a keen judge of life. He was deeply moved by the absence of civil rights, the humiliation of the poor by the rich, class antagonisms, envy and the dishonors of that time. For this reason his works were filled with humanistic ideas."[75]

Ravjaa's most spell-binding parable-poem was titled 'The Kite.' The work was created in 1825 when Ravjaa was just 22 years old and is one of his best-known writings.

It follows the tune of a popular song of the day and includes old religious philosophies and quotations taken from folklore. It is in fact a moral tale categorized as one of Ravjaa's 19 teaching poems.

According to the parable, a person from a border area dreams one night of a man flying a paper kite. In the dream, the man lets the kite fly away and is then visited by the border man who questions his life, ambitions and purpose. According to Tibetan tradition, a border person is also uncouth, uneducated, barbaric, or at least without religion – hence the need to gain instruction from the kite-flyer.

The story begins with a question.

"Is it easy to make this kite?" the border man asks the kite flier.

The other responds, "Yes, it is easy."

"What else is easy to do?" the man asks.

"Bad deeds are easy," says the other.

"What are there very few of?" the man asks.

"People who do not defend themselves, of those there are few," the man responds.

"What are there many of?" the man asks.

"Careless people with a bad fate," the other says.

"What is ugly?" he then asks.

"The ignorant ones are ugly," says the other.

"What is beautiful?" he then asks.

"A clear mind is beautiful," says the other.

"What is harmful?" he asks.

"Hateful thoughts are harmful," says the other.

"What is useful?"

"A good mind is useful," answers the other.

"What is deception?"

"This life is deception."

"And what is true?"

"The Three Jewels are true."

"And what is evil?"

"The lack of dharma is evil."

"And what is good?" he then asks.

"Courage is good," says the other.

"And what is the nature of man in this time?"

"Oh woe, to ponder the character of the people of the present time, it is as if one tears apart the rope which connects us to this world. When they make offerings to the Three Jewels they feel as if it is a burden. When they listen to teachings they feel imposed upon.

"People making friends with monks slowly make them their slaves. They (are selfish and) would guard everything that belongs to them, even if it was a dog. They (don't care for others and) would leave anything that belongs to others even if it was Buddha.

"They behave nicely with one who is rich even if they are an enemy. They would even leave their own parents if they were poor. If it promises gain they would make their body slaves. They escape from good karma if they have no courage. They would praise even a thief if they fell in love. They would have friendship with devils if there were a partnership. I cannot describe all this badness of this Universe."

He concludes by saying, "To be brief, being tied by the karmic rope in the prison of the Universe (samsara) and being drunk by attachment in the darkness of ignorance, cut by the knife of anger, burned by pride, gone mad with jealousy, tortured by the suffering world!

"Pity on all of them, those poor living beings. Life without essence, the savior rope is cut. The eye that sees what should be abandoned and cultivated is blinded. Pity on them, all these poor living beings."

Then the man asks – "In such a bad time, what direction should one take to find truth?"

The other answers, "Though being watchful is one's best friend, do not be suspicious of your lama, father, mother or Three Jewels. Though being friendly is the highest skill, do not befriend people with bad karma. Though it is tradition to talk in a meeting, do not talk too much.

"There is no refuge higher than Buddha, so keep your faith and do not become suspicious. There is no wisdom higher than the Dharma, so learn it and do not take pride. There is no support higher than Sangha, so respect Sangha and do not try to find fault."[76]

The excerpt is followed by continued teachings of Dharma, as well as more personal stanzas. Ravjaa then writes, "Many false and true words are written here for the purpose of entertainment," indicating a sense of playful humility.

These breaks in the action indicate that Ravjaa was somehow writing the piece while falling in and out of mood swings or bouts of drunkenness. But the passage does more than entertain. It educates on morality, the need for honesty and the importance of piousness.

The piece is befitting of Ravjaa's contradictory nature. Here was a man of wild habits that could step into the shoes of propriety when it came time to write. For Ravjaa, writing was a fantasy world in which he could express the peace and calm that he so longed for. Words gave him an outlet for pleasure and goodness. Likewise, Ravjaa also reflected on himself negatively through his words. He must surely have been speaking of himself when he wrote, "There is no hell, but if you perform bad deeds you will create your own hell." Such a statement was a warning to himself, as much as to others, that the illusion of hell could be created by negative thoughts or deeds.

The anti-Manchu monks that raised Ravjaa in Inner Mongolia perhaps influenced his precepts and critiques, just as Ravjaa influenced other writers who came after him. It is probable that the Inner Mongolian poet and novelist Injanashi (1837-1891) studied Ravjaa's works and incorporated them into his own teachings. Injanashi, an eccentric historian, wrote a prose saga called *Khökh Sudur* (Blue Chronicle) which condemns those Mongols who had lost their identity and instead studied Chinese culture and history. Injanashi praised the efforts of Chinggis Khaan and ordered all Mongols to respect his spiritual authority and unite in the face of Chinese aggression. The book, however, was not published until long after the author's death and failed to have much of an impact.[77]

Another monk who perhaps followed in Ravjaa's footsteps was a certain Dandar, who was highly critical of the Seventh Bogd Gegeen in his 1860 text, *The Thunderbolt which Crushes the Thorns of the Evil-Doers*. The text, which follows in part, is even more direct than the criticisms Danzan Ravjaa leveled at the Buddhist hierarchy.

"It is indeed pitiful how the incarnations and nobles go shamelessly after profit, lechery and drink, like dogs that have tasted blood… These ostensible lamas sit on the heads of the people, torturing them with the spurs on their feet… They pay no heed either to the scriptures of the law, pursuing their evil ways at their own sweet will."[78]

Just how much of Ravjaa's works actually circulated in Mongolia, and the effect they had on the writers who followed, is unknown. But his criticisms of society seem to have outlasted those made by his contemporaries. Certainly his poetry is studied now more than ever before. His written words have struck a chord with modern Mongolians seeking social change and a reformation to the ills of their troubled society. The following is a short collection of Ravjaa's best-known poetry.

Pleasures of High Summertime

Let me sing my words of truth
As a gift of this day's gathering
In the beauty of your good manner
And pleasure of fine summertime

In the soft wind of autumn
When the leaves and flowers sway
When meadows and grasses flutter and ripple
I think of you the only one

When the cuckoo of joyous summer sings
When I see folks of my age
Your beautiful and gentle manners
Turns more and more towards me

The mist that spreads out
When the geese just flew back
And new clouds pile up
All this suddenly moved my feelings

In the faraway land that seems to turn blue
The mirage of geese struggle to move
And the breath of the clear lake
Moves my calm mind

In this my feeling of missing you
Clear as the moon
The words you said when we met
Are sharp as starlight

In this human body which was found,
In this life which is so easy to lose
The darkness of desires that makes one ignorant,
Makes one lost – this is the nature of the world.

In the intensity of youth
Thanks to you we met in this life
In the light of clear emptiness,
May we meet on the path to Nirvana[79]

Through the Eight Directions

The way lotus leaves
Sway through the eight directions,
The swaying of the leaf

Like the behavior of the narrow river,
My only companion

Like the *pi-wang*'s sweet melody,
Your song enchants me
With elegant words.
She is honorable and beautiful
More special than others

The way she was born
With a holy virgin smell,
The scent of your lover.
This scent will come from far away,
You will most certainly feel excitement

Like the pure water of heaven,
It brings sweet desires.
And your way is lovely,
You hold my grasping mind,
Like the moon on the fifteenth day

Like the blazing hot sun
You open the lotus to life.
You eliminate wild darkness.
I shall stay close to Padmasambhava,
I shall be joyful and happy[80]

The Five Signs

The hot wind just blew
Each place thawed out

Migrating birds are here
Signs of springtime

The sun just rose
The rain has fallen
Grass and plants have awoken
Signs of summertime

The fine wind blew
Leaves and flowers become yellow
Drove back the ones with fine voices[81]
Signs of autumn

The thick clouds came out
And covered the high Khangai
The clouds' snow fell down
Signs of wintertime

The midday sun sinks
Youthful age passed
Thick hair becomes gray
Signs of aging

The name of this song
Is the 'Five Signs'
The precious Noyon Hutagt
Has created and sung it with melody[82]

Topaz
Great is the wisdom of topaz,

Great is the happiness of the Mongol lands.
Great is the assistance of horse and camel
Great is the need for firewood

Nothing is plentiful when all is exhausted
Nothing is believable when someone laughs
Nothing offers nourishment when you've eaten
Nothing is helpful in scholarship

Far is the length of the springtime journey
Far away is pleasure for a mind that's dissatisfied
Far on the horizon lies the Khangai
Far away are the friends of a jealous man

Foolish it is to teach those who lack understanding
Foolish it is to joke with those who are irascible
Foolish it is to hang around with those without stability
Foolish it is to encourage those whose minds lack emotion

A sign of loyalty is to criticize without reserve
A sign of wisdom is to consider deeply
A sign of a lover is to talk without secrets
A sign of friendship is to have similar thoughts

May the lives of our superiors be long
And may the lives of our friends be full
May the suffering of beings be pacified in the world
And may we take pleasure in openness and wonder[83]

8

THE RENAISSANCE MAN

"Danzan Ravjaa was a genius and a prophet who understood the secrets of nature. He was a fortune-teller, he could stop wars and he could create rain to end drought. His poetry was the basis for modern Mongolian writers. Danzan Ravjaa composed melodies and poems, directed dances, and built cultural centers. He is not just a renaissance man in Mongolia, but unique among men in the world."[84]

D. Baatar, Khamaryn Khiid Lama

During the later years of Ravjaa's life, June 15th every year witnessed a special ceremony on a knoll near Khamaryn Khiid. Women would gather on the hill in the morning, encircle two *ovoo* symbolizing female breasts, and flick milk into the air with spoons. While women came to the site to purify themselves and honor the spirits, men could only come to visit after the death of their mother.

This celebration was a particular honor for women at that time, given the usual Mongol tradition of forbidding women to climb to the top of sacred hills and mountains.

"Breast Ovoo," built by Danzan Ravjaa, is symbolic of an

important value he imposed on his disciples: the equality of women. One drives by the site even today on the road into Khamaryn Khiid.

"Danzan Ravjaa was the first writer to bring love and women close to ordinary people," said Tumorbaatar, a professor at the Mongolian National University, and a researcher of Ravjaa's poetry. He continued, "His goal was to elevate the status of the lower class by showing that, even if they didn't have the wealth of the aristocracy, everyone has similar emotions. Rich or poor, every person can experience love and hate, joy and sorrow."

Ravjaa states in his autobiography that his first sexual encounter was with a middle-aged woman who acted as his instructor. He was 15 years old at the time. The incident may have been his first lesson in secret tantric practices. Ravjaa did not believe that these practices should be concealed.

"Ravjaa's instructions on tantra showed his disciples how to get in touch with sensitive mental points. It is a deep philosophy, understandable only to highly educated people," explains Mongolian artist G. Tsagaanderem, another researcher of Danzan Ravjaa's artistic endeavors. "If you can understand the prayers associated with each position of male-female tantra then maybe you could fly, walk through walls or remember things that happened when you slept or even in your previous lifetimes."

The equality granted to women in Ravjaa's monasteries became a trademark of sorts. Soon aristocrats and nobles from Korea, Japan, China and Tibet began sending their best female students to study at his Gobi monasteries. Legendary stories tell how the number of young women sent to him eventually reached 108, an auspicious number according to Buddhist tradition. The exact nature of the relationship Ravjaa shared with these women is unknown. Some were tantric partners while others remained students. Their presence at Ravjaa's monasteries, however, caused anxiety among other leaders. Malicious rumors about his behavior spread in Huree, where Ravjaa was particularly unpopular.

Two women, Dadishura and Baljudmaa, were considered his 'wives' although this term should be used carefully as no formal marriage between them ever took place. Dadishura, who came from the region around Erdene Zuu monastery in central Mongolia, was the more prominent of the two and considered an intellectual equal to Ravjaa. She wrote music, she choreographed plays and she worked in Ravjaa's traveling theater group. The year of her birth is unknown but she was probably older than Ravjaa, since he referred to her as his 'aunt.' It's entirely possible that it was Dadishura who acted as Ravjaa's first tantric instructor when he was 15.

If Dadishura was Ravjaa's yin, then Baljudmaa was his yang. This young beauty had extraordinary grace and seductive powers. She came from the cool Khangai Mountains, famed for producing the most beautiful women in Mongolia. It was her radiant looks that inspired so many of Ravjaa's love poems. Ravjaa met Baljudmaa (some sources call her Sogtzuul) on a visit to Huree in 1840. Captivated by her beauty and charm, he traveled to her homeland in Arkhangai where they spent the summer together. Baljudmaa gave birth to a boy, who Ravjaa named Dunkhor, one of perhaps several illegitimate children. Danzan Ravjaa writes about his son in the poem *My Fine Cream White Horse*:

> The sandalwood tree
> Is fixed, not rigid

My son has a destiny
To learn without instruction

The coconut tree
Is dark brown and solid
My son has a gift
To learn without difficulty[85]

Dunkhor was sent to a monastery in modern-day Arkhangai Aimag at a young age and was recognized by elder lamas as a huvilgan. He was known as the 'Hutagt of Tamir' and was renowned for his singing ability. Dunkhor kept a collection of over 300 songs describing the beauty of Arkhangai Aimag and the longing for a lost lover. It is presumed that his father wrote these songs. Dunkhor lived more than 80 years, dying shortly after the 1921 Communist Revolution.

The fact that Danzan Ravjaa had fathered a child may have caused alarm among some Buddhist leaders, but what seemed more troublesome was that Ravjaa allowed the monks and nuns at his monastery to worship and live together. Ignoring these complaints, Ravjaa wrote, "Everyone is born of the same blood, so let this blood mix. It is true that even the Buddhas join their flesh together. Men and women live together; this is the law of nature. One cannot go against nature."[86] Danzan Ravjaa was clearly looking beyond the traditions of Buddhism, seeking to break down its barriers and thus reform it.

Despite his suggestions that opposites can co-exist, Ravjaa's decisions were not always followed. Pressure from the Gelugpa caused many of the Khamaryn Khiid monks to segregate themselves from the nuns. According to the legend, influenza spread within the living quarters at Khamaryn Khiid after the men and women were separated. When asked why they had been afflicted with the disease, Ravjaa explained that the separation of the sexes had offended the female Buddha-protector of Khamaryn Khiid, the Amaa Buddha.

"He respected women and showed that they could be educated and skilled. In fact, many of the nuns of Khamaryn Khiid were considered more powerful than their male counterparts. That was shocking for people in those days; they were not used to seeing men and women working together, or seeing women so respected. His lesson made Gobi people more reverent to women,"[87] explains museum curator Altangerel.

Continuing the tradition of prayer to Amaa, Altangerel organized a special ceremony for the deity when the monastery re-opened in 1990. Since then, the monks at Khamaryn Khiid have taken a very liberal approach to their views of women. "Women can give as much to Buddhism as any male lama. Their minds are open, free and willing to accept the Buddha's teaching. Danzan Ravjaa pressed this upon all his disciples,"[88] says Dösh, the abbot at Khamaryn Khiid.

While Ravjaa expressed his appreciation for women and their intellectual abilities, he likewise expressed his disregard for aggressive men. There is a fable related to this called the "Drunken Men of Gobi Mergen Van Hoshuu," and along with providing a moral, it gives us more insight into the unique and creative minds of 19th-century Mongol storytellers.

The story describes how alcohol-related violence was increasing in the region, much to the dismay of local leaders and the women of the hoshuu. The Regional Governor Lasurenbazar was at a loss at how to quell the situation and called on Danzan Ravjaa for assistance. Ravjaa agreed to help pacify the people and made an announcement that all men should gather for a special theatrical performance. Crowds of drunken men were soon assembled before the main temple, eager to see the Hutagt's performance.

Ravjaa appeared on the roof of the temple and called for the attention of the drunks. As a show of his powers, he pulled open his robes and urinated on the roof. His urine trickled over the edge, but then magically flowed right back up to the temple roof before hitting the ground. This is similar to a story told about the sixth Dalai Lama, who urinated from the roof of the Potala Palace and just before it hit the ground, returned the urine back to the roof.

The drunks were astounded. The Hutagt then called down to the men, "If any of you can perform such a feat, climb up here and show us." No one moved; they were too terrified of the great monk. Ravjaa spoke again, "You are all so weak and small compared to me! So why do you behave with such wildness? You behave like a male goat in the autumn! You must put an end to this abhorrent behavior, stop drinking and stop insulting women."

Ravjaa climbed down from the roof and assembled the drunkards around a dining table. He announced that a meal was being provided in their honor. Each was then served a large bowl of hot, steaming dog feces. "Please eat and drink!" he said. They refused and said they would never eat the feces. Ravjaa grew angry again. "Aren't you all like dogs?" he bellowed. "Because you are drunks you eat whatever scraps of food that you find in your hand. So why don't you eat the food that has been placed before you? Why are you refusing to eat it?"

The Hutagt breathed deeply and spoke again. "Now you understand that you are flesh and blood and your body is all you have, so don't punish it with vodka." Ravjaa then chanted a prayer and the dog excrement turned into wonderful, sweet-smelling fruit. Following this god-like show of power, there was no more violence or abuse of alcohol and women.[89]

This is one Danzan Ravjaa legend that does indeed have historical basis. The story is likely to stem from an incident in 1852, in the wake of the Taiping Rebellion, when rebels were still on the run in China and threatened the peace and stability of Outer Mongolia. Noblemen from Tushet Khaan Aimag and Tsetsen Khaan Aimag, as well as Manchurian officials, feared that the rebels would stir up trouble in Mongolia and asked Danzan Ravjaa to conduct a religious ceremony to keep the rebels out of their territories. Ravjaa agreed and completed the prayers. For years afterwards Gobi people believed their land had been protected from the civil war by Danzan Ravjaa's prayers.

* * *

In addition to Ravjaa's many talents as an artist and lover, he was also said to be a skilled medical practitioner and medicine maker. Wherever he traveled, Ravjaa took with him herbal medicines to cure the sick. Some came to him on horseback from distant areas, seeking medicine and advice. Fabulous legends also tell of Ravjaa curing the sick from great distances by using mental telepathy and prayers in all manner and form. A favorite story told by Dösh, the abbot of Khamaryn Khiid, describes a distraught father whose son has fallen gravely ill. One day, the man decides to meet Danzan Ravjaa in hopes of curing his son. After explaining the circumstances of his visit, Ravjaa ducked inside his ger and returned with a flintlock gun. Positioning the heavy gun towards the man's ger, a full 60 kilometers away, Ravjaa took careful aim and fired. The shot rang out and a plume of smoke rose from the barrel of his crude weapon. Ravjaa put away his gun and said "Go home now, your child is better."

Confused, frightened and bewildered, the man mounted his horse and rode home. Upon arrival he found his child completely revived, healthy-looking and in good spirits. There was also a gaping hole in the ger wall. "How did that happen?" the man asked his wife.

"We were just sitting here when we heard the sound of guns," the wife said. "Then the ger wall collapsed. Our son started vomiting pus, and now he is better!"

"A flintlock gun can only shoot 800 meters but Danzan Ravjaa could shoot 60 kilometers for the purpose of healing others. This was the power of his Buddhist healing abilities,"[90] Dösh Lama explained.

Ravjaa's eccentric methods for healing did not stop there. He also employed the use of *chod*, a type of tantric practice used to heal his patients. Chod dates back to 12th-century Tibet, where it was developed by a mystical woman named Machig Labdrön. It begins when a practitioner visualizes his or her physical body cut up and transformed into white and red food. The white food is for the pacific spirits and red is for the violent and demonic forces. The food is then offered to all beings, to the whole universe, to satisfy their cravings and bring them enlightenment. In this way the practitioner loses attachment to his or her physical body.

According to one legend in which Danzan Ravjaa employs chod healing, a grief-stricken mother and father brought their gravely sick child to Ravjaa. When they entered the great monk's ger they found him drunk, a bottle of booze in one hand and a naked young woman in the other. Embarrassed and disappointed, the couple excused themselves and asked to be let out. But Ravjaa refused and demanded to know why they had come to his ger. Thus they told the story of how their child had become mortally ill and that no other monks could heal him.

Ravjaa asked the couple to set the boy on the table, which they did. Slowly he rose in his drunkenness, grabbed a steel sword and cut off one of the boy's arms. Horrified, the mother and father watched Ravjaa fling their child's bloody arm under a bed. He did the same to the other arm, and then to both his legs. Finally, he decapitated the boy and rolled the head under his furniture. Ravjaa then instructed the grief-stricken mother and father to return in two days, at which time they could collect their boy.

The shocked parents left the ger consoling one another but still followed Ravjaa's instructions and returned on the appointed day. Again they found Ravjaa drunk, lying on his bed with a naked girl. He asked why they had come, slurring as he spoke and angry at being awakened in the early morning. When the parents reminded him that he had dismembered and decapitated their child Ravjaa recalled their previous visit.

Stumbling out of bed, Ravjaa reached under the furniture, picking up the torso, four limbs and the head. Setting the various bits of human anatomy on his workbench, Ravjaa began fitting the pieces together as though the child were a broken toy. This imagery may have been familiar to shamans who at a young age are taken by the spirits, torn limb from limb, and reassembled. But it's more likely that the story, theatrical as it may sound, has closer links to the chod tantric practice.

At last Ravjaa replaced the boy's head on the torso, uttered a prayer, and brought him back to life. "Your boy is now healthy again and you may leave," Ravjaa told the family.[91]

A little bit of humor resonates through many of these Danzan Ravjaa healing legends. Take for example the tale of the 'sacrificial domino.' The story must be prefaced with the knowledge that in Mongolia a domino with four dots is called 'Yods,' and a domino with two dots is called 'Yods huu,' son of the Yods.

According to the story, a worried man goes to a famed Tibetan lama-astrologer and asks about the fate of his ill brother. The lama consults his astrological instruments and determines that the brother will die after one week and there is no cure for his ailment. The man is distraught but decides that he needs a second opinion and thus pays a visit to Danzan Ravjaa.

Upon arriving at Khamaryn Khiid the man finds Ravjaa in a courtyard playing dominoes. He is ashamed to disturb Ravjaa, particularly since he already consulted another lama. So he waits. Finally, without any prompting, Ravjaa asks the man about his brother.

"He is very sick, hutagt. But how did you…"

"I can read your thoughts," said Ravjaa. "The Tibetan lama you met before was correct, there is no cure for your brother. He will be dead in a week. However, the Tibetan does not know how to save your brother. There is a way." And with that he went back to his game of dominoes.

The man waits, believing that Danzan Ravjaa would explain how his brother could be saved. But Ravjaa said nothing. Instead, he picked up a domino, a 'Yods huu' domino with two dots, held it aloft for a moment, then slams it to the table saying, "Yods huu, you should die instead of this man's brother!" There was a resounding 'clack' as the domino hit the table. The man was understandably perplexed. He thinks Ravjaa might be telling a joke, but the hutagt does not laugh. Ravjaa ignores him thereafter, so the man goes home distraught.

As the days passed the brother's health showed signs of improvement. Miraculously, he was still alive after a week. The man thus returned to the Tibetan lama for an explanation. The Tibetan again consulted his instruments. Spreading out pebbles and bones on the floor he studied their arrangement like tarot cards and was amazed to see that the brother was indeed still alive.

"I see that somebody named Yods Huu has died instead of your brother! What a great sacrifice he has made, to die for your brother out of compassion. Do you know this Yods Huu? Does he live in your home area?"

The Tibetan of course would not have understood the Mongolian domino reference and the listener gets a laugh at his expense. Fortunately, the man's brother is also saved.[92]

Although such stories are pure legend, this sort of telepathic and mystical healing employed by Ravjaa was actually quite popular among tantric practitioners. Even those who did not use tantra still had many uses for the "healing prayer." It is believed that prayers and chants can cure 101 different types of disease. In most cases the prayers are read aloud in the presence of the sick, as a sort of exorcism to drive the bad spirits from the patient's body. In some cases, a prayer would actually be written down on paper and swallowed.

Ravjaa composed several healing prayers. He used them frequently on his patients, who often included senior monks such as the Bogd Gegeen. One of the prayers was designed specifically for children, to which there is a legend attached.

Danzan Ravjaa had tried in vain for several months to compose the healing song, growing more and more frustrated with his writer's block. One night he was staying with a wealthy family on a trip away from his monastery. A feast of colossal proportions was prepared, and the family got to bed late after enjoying their hearty meal.

While sound asleep, a loud wailing outside the felt tent awaked Ravjaa. He was so saddened by the cries that he could not sleep. "The sorrowful voice began with a wail, dragged on to become a 'long song' and finished with misery and affliction," Ravjaa said.

After some moments of rest the song began anew, each time with more lamentable cries. Ravjaa lost his patience, got out of bed, threw on his saffron robe, and trudged out into the night. The family, meanwhile, did not stir from their peaceful, wine-induced slumber.

Ravjaa climbed a nearby hill, sat down and listened to the song. By daybreak his heart was weeping with sorrow and when the song ended, he had it memorized. This was the song of a she-wolf that had lost her cub. With this inspiration, Ravjaa was able to compose his prayer for the child.

It is said that anyone who listened to this sorrowful sounding melody would cry. The song, remarkably, can also induce the birth of a child. It is, of course, the melody and tone of the song that are essential for the prayer's effectiveness; the words are almost meaningless. Even so, it requires the expert singing of a spiritually advanced lama for the prayer to bring results. We can think of this as a lullaby. It's easy to fall asleep to soft, melodic singing, no matter what the language or lyrics. It was this theory that Buddhists applied to their healing prayers.

*   *   *

While melody was crucial to Danzan Ravjaa's songs, it is his fine lyrics that transcend time and culture. He used universal themes that are appealing today, one of which was the horse. Titles like 'My Fine Cream White Horse,' 'Lovely Rangy Brown,' 'Your Lovely Sandalwood Horse,' and 'My Strong, Swift Brown' are all dedicated to his favorite steeds. He often draws parallels between a proud horse and a lovely woman and often uses the horse as a symbol of freedom. In the following poem, *Tishgedelt Kheer* (Chestnut Steps), Ravjaa describes the love he has for his wife and his rush to see her. But at the same time he takes much pleasure in describing the horses he rides on his return home. One wonders which he truly favors more.

Taking from the group of horses
My chestnut, pacing
Showing off nearby
I'll pass the time with my angry wife

I shall pass the summer training
My wild chestnut mare
She'll be trotting out nearby
As I pass the time with my interesting wife

They're growing dark and misty
Our territory and yours
Our one love
Residing in place

The mountains of the Khangai
Darken into night blue
One love, alas
Residing in place

A group of many horses
And I take all the spirited ones.
Now I shall go back,
Please don't remember too much

And please, don't forget
How I am honest.
And please don't hurry to ride away
Surely the day is long, please do not go away fast

It is scarcely possible to forget
Such a loving mind.
By the blessing of the Dalai Lama
May we be happy together, everywhere[93]

In addition to writing odes about them, Ravjaa was also a keen horse trainer. A short dissertation on horse training, written by Ravjaa and still in print, describes what traits trainers must be aware of before racing a horse. Bristling chest fur and leg spasms three days before the race are positive signs. A horse will lose a race, he wrote, if its teeth are yellowing, if it frequently bites people or other horses, has a darkened shade of face color, a wrinkled nose, a large stomach or a loss of fur. To write such a book might seem rather unconventional for a monk but as we have seen, Danzan Ravjaa's pursuits reached well beyond Buddhism.

Aside from training horses, Ravjaa also took time to educate herders how to care for their livestock, barter their goods with passing caravan men and use natural resources to their fullest extent. Not only did he lecture in front of audiences, he also founded schools, museums and libraries to continue the legacy of his teachings.

The establishment of an education center stemmed from his personal collection of foreign art and treasure, which grew to become a well-known museum. Included in his collection were Buddhist icons presented by the Dalai Lama, Manchurian rulers, the banner chiefs of China, and the princes of Korea and Japan. Of his many curios, it was said that his most prized possession was the head and skin of the Yeti, known in Mongolia as 'Almas.'

The mythical Almas is described by Gobi people as standing about seven feet tall and covered with a fine coat of red fur. Ravjaa described this creature as an "absent-minded marmot-eating beast." He acquired the skin and head from a wandering monk named Luvsandonoi. This monk had been traveling to Mongolia from Tibet when he found several dead Almas lying in the snow. He cut the skin off one and collected its bile (the bile was sold to the personal physician of the seventh Bogd Gegeen in Huree). Danzan Ravjaa acquired the skin and kept it at his monastery Galbiin Ulaan Sakhosnii Khiid. In 1961, an elderly man by the name of Luvsondash reported his memories of what this monastery looked like before its destruction in 1937. Luvsondash told researchers from the Mongolian National University that the temple contained "a human-like skin that was covered in hair."[94]

In 1842, Ravjaa built a special temple to house his most precious artifacts; the Givaadin Ravjaaling Treasury was probably Mongolia's first museum. Inside the building, around the marble walls, were five white stone statues of shapely goddesses. In the hands of these female deities were lamps (*möngön tsogts*) which gave off a white glow. Hence, the visitors to this shrine called it the "White Temple."

The most important of the 10,000-plus exhibits at the White Temple was a horsehair banner that once, allegedly, flew over 13th-century Mongol armies. The museum also held a small statue of the Indian poet Nagarjuna, which was supposedly cast in England. The exhibits were placed in a particular order so that natural items, minerals and plants were shown first as the visitor entered the museum. A large statue of a woman in the nude was towards the front, symbolizing the natural state of human beings.

A storage room attached to the museum housed the bulk of its belongings in large leather-bound boxes. Because Ravjaa was concerned that goods from his monastery could be stolen or confiscated by Manchu authorities, these boxes were carefully stored so that they could be easily moved onto the backs of camels and evacuated. In one instance, this well-executed pre-arranged plan apparently foiled a real robbery attempt by brigands.

Ravjaa sometimes acted as a museum guide, but his two *gomiir*, or caretakers, usually handled this task. One was a lama responsible for educating visitors on philosophy and religious topics. The other, a layperson, explained exhibits related to science and nature. The gomiir were charged with preserving the objects and used several techniques to do so. Cloth was protected from moths by a liquid made from crushed sagebrush and wormwood. Artwork was protected from fading with the application of cow bile mixed with water. Wood exhibits were boiled in oil and water, and then stored in wooden boxes filled with cow and horse dung.

As the museum grew, so did its importance as an educational center. Admission was free and assistants were on hand to read the textbooks to illiterate nomads. In exchange, visitors left a blue silk scarf (*khadak*). Ravjaa also hosted cultural competitions at the museum. Artists and poets competed with one another for the sake of honor. Winners were called 'Duvchin' and given a special place to sit inside the White Temple. They also received an engraved wood seal known as a *paiz*, which granted them the right to teach at other monasteries in Mongolia.

"The White Temple was a real cultural center. It even had training courses for people who wanted to learn to read and write. The idea was that if you went there you became a sacred person," wrote researcher Ts. Tsendsuren.[95]

The museum was only one part of a larger project to educate laypeople. The library at Khamaryn Khiid was also a landmark in Mongolia. It contained tens of thousands of books, both lay and religious. Eight lamas, five translators and 13 assistants were on hand to read the texts, most of which were in Tibetan script. Like the museum, the library was not restricted to the elite, but open to the general public, who could spend time with the assistants asking them questions and reading the available materials. Equally impressive was the so-called 'Children's Temple,' which existed well into the 20th century and was known for its intensive training, progressive teaching methods and variety of classes, including language, history, math, dance, art and singing. The classes even had their own coursework; some of the material was created or commissioned by Danzan Ravjaa, including a text called *Alphabet for Teaching and Memorizing the Law of Living,* which gave instructions on language and grammar.

Most monasteries in Mongolia offered youth education, but the seminary at Khamaryn Khiid was believed to be one of the largest and most advanced of its time. It offered free education to children regardless of their sex or class distinctions.[96]

Pen and ink block

9

ADVENTURES AND COMPANIONS

As a poet who loved to travel and study the theater of other cultures, the stories about Danzan Ravjaa's adventures abroad are well known. Although many seem fictional, most are based on real journeys to China and parts of Outer Mongolia. Ravjaa's own contemporaries even recognized him as a brave adventurer, exemplified in 1831 when noblemen of Alasha compared him to the Chan-masters of old Chinese folk tales, such as the eccentric Chi-Tien (Jidian or Crazy Ji), the hero of a novel titled Chi-Kung Chuan.[97] The nobles came to this conclusion after they found Ravjaa mysteriously excavating the Agui Süm, mentioned in chapter three of this book. Baffled by the behavior of this drunken, apparently sex-crazed monk, they decided to challenge his supposed brilliance.

"Test this newcomer from the Gobi who is accompanied by women and pupils. Test him on his strengths of faith," they said to Smonlam Rav Byamba Naavangstandar, a famed linguist and genius who was native to the Alasha region. He accepted their challenge and went to visit Ravjaa's camp, where he found the hutagt drinking brandy. "Please take some," Ravjaa offered. But as a yellow hat monk, the linguist waved off the drink with defiance.

He then raised a finger and inquired, "Are there devils?"

"If one believes in devils then they exist. If you do not believe in devils then they do not exist," Ravjaa answered.

The linguist then asked, "Is there a master Buddha?" to which Ravjaa responded with equal vagueness, "In truth it is true; as a lie, it's a lie."

Growing more impressed by the moment by these philosophical answers, the linguist finally asks, "After a human has died, does he return again as a human?" to which Ravjaa gave his final answer, "A human is born from a human, but whether a human is reborn from another human, I do not know." And, at such brilliance, the linguist retired back to the homes of the noblemen, to whom he reported his "defeat to the drunken genius of the Gobi."[98]

This is but one of many legendary stories about Ravjaa's adventures and travels. Other stories describe how such activities were restricted by order of the Manchus, who did not want the popular monk rabble-rousing. In 1850, legend says, the Emperor of China ordered Ravjaa to serve as a doctor in his army, with the real intention of separating him from his followers. When the Emperor learned that Danzan Ravjaa was to join the troops bearing a Mongol black banner, he ordered him to also bear a Manchu yellow banner. Ravjaa did as he was told and carried the yellow banner south. En route to his destination, however, he mended the Manchu banner by placing red cloth over the yellow and decorating it with the Soyombo, a symbol of the first Bogd Gegeen Zanabazar. It was such overt acts of rebellion like this one that continued to add to his legend.[99]

"The Manchus did not appreciate Ravjaa because he educated his people and opened their eyes to the reality of the world and the injustices of society. If the people knew the truth about their country it would cause instability. This is why he was separated from them,"[100] notes researcher D. Bold.

While many legends tell of Danzan Ravjaa's conflicts with the Emperor, there is but one instance of him siding with China. According to the tale, Ravjaa volunteered for the Emperor's army between 1839 and 1842, during the First Opium War. He contributed to the war effort, legend says, by conjuring up thunderstorms to damage the British fleet. He sent lightning bolts in the direction of their ships and had the ability to make ten Chinese soldiers look like a thousand, giving them a menacing appearance when they stood off against the British army. Yet, according to the story, Ravjaa lamented that even his powers could not help the Chinese, whose negative karma to lose the war was greater than his magic abilities.[101]

Did Ravjaa really meet the Emperor? While most people of the Gobi believe he did, the truth remains unknown.

We are left with one curious legend about a meeting between the Son of Heaven and the Son of the Steppes. According to the tale, the Bogd Khaan dispatched Ravjaa to Peking as a representative of his government. The Bogd wanted to protest the increasing number of Chinese settlers arriving in Outer Mongolia and asked Ravjaa to oppose this threat to Mongolia.

Ravjaa agreed and traveled to Peking as a senior diplomat. During the meeting, the Emperor proved to be inflexible on many issues that concerned Ravjaa. He pushed Ravjaa hard on the population issue, insisting that the relocation of Chinese settlers would not cease.

Ravjaa decided to cool off the arrogant Emperor. In his hand he held a cup of wine that was half full. Tilting the cup towards the south, the wine came right to the rim of the cup. At that moment the earth in all of Peking tilted to the south and created much havoc.

"What are you doing?" the Sovereign exclaimed, nearly falling out of his throne. "Stop this at once!"

Danzan Ravjaa stopped the earth from shaking, but the tremor was enough to make the Emperor apologize for his aggressive behavior. To this day, the Mongols say, Beijing remains tilted towards the south.

Such incidents and adventures allowed Ravjaa to come to conclusions about foreigners and gave him perspective on his own people. He once recorded that, "The Chinese feeds himself with grass because he was born from the dragon. He is full of passion, knows no shame, is very careful, greedy and thinking of profit. The Tibetan feeds himself with flour because he was born from bad ghosts. He has no shame, is quick in wit, is very jealous and is full of bad plans. The Mongol eats meat because he was born from giants who ate people. He is proud, enjoys chatting, has little education or knowledge, and is very eager to attack his opponent."[102]

It is entirely possible that on one of these journeys in China, Danzan Ravjaa met the French missionary, the Abbé Huc. While the theory may be optimistic, their paths may have crossed at a guesthouse in a town called Chuang Lang, around the year 1844. In his book, the Frenchman describes his meeting with a Living Buddha of about 50 years of age. Huc wrote that the huvilgan was "comfortably stout; his dark brown face denoted extreme good nature, but there was in his eyes, when you attentively examined them, a strange wild, haggard expression that was very alarming."

The age and description match Danzan Ravjaa perfectly, but unfortunately Huc does not tell his readers the name of this

mysterious Buddha. This anonymous monk and the Abbé Huc
sat down for a long chat. At first the monk was wary of sitting on
the same level as a "mere mortal," but he conceded, overcome by
curiosity. After small talk, the huvilgan examined the Abbé Huc's
breviary, and touched it to his forehead respectfully.

He then punched his fists together and said, "Your religion
and ours are like this." The Frenchman then admitted that he
was a missionary with a goal to convert Chinese and Mongols to
Christianity.

The huvilgan leafed through the book again and asked for
explanations of the engravings. Upon hearing about the crucifixion,
he shook his head compassionately.

They met again later that same day for another talk, during
which time Huc described his origin. The huvilgan, unfamiliar
with France, commented that one's origin mattered not – since all
men are brothers. Before parting, Huc again comments that the
lama appeared somehow "infernal and fiend-like," but added with
respect that he was "a most amiable personage."[103]

Although we do not know the name of this huvilgan, we can
see that this monk was skeptical of foreigners. Sources say Danzan
Ravjaa was also xenophobic and harbored great fear about foreign
occupation of Mongolia. Chinese and Russians were coming to the
Gobi to study and map the land, and Ravjaa watched them with
mistrust. Oral legend has him identifying "spies of nine languages."
Ravjaa specifically feared Russian archaeologists, believing them to
be 'grave robbers.'

There is a story attached to this. It tells how Ravjaa fought the
'foreign devils' by casting a shamanic spell upon them. He sacrificed
a hornless black bull at a place called Ulaan Ovoo, mixed together
its blood and cud, and read a prayer called "Khandain Magdag."

The prayer incited the spirit of the ovoo to blow strong, horrible winds across the Gobi, raking the land with sandstorms that made work impossible for the foreign 'spies.' Some suffered from hallucinations and were sent back to their homeland, deranged and mad.[104]

Nineteenth-century Mongolia was not an easy period for any type of travel, and Ravjaa's wealthy entourage invited brigands and bandits. Included in his drama company were 20 or 30 women and around ten men, including students, teachers and performers. Such a large and well endowed group would have been a popular target for thieves.

Legends speak of Ravjaa's bravery in the face of bandit attacks. During one robbery attempt it is said that he leapt down from the caravan wagon and single-handedly slew seven or eight bandits, using the martial arts skills he picked up from Chinese martial arts experts. Upon witnessing this display of heroism, a Japanese student presented Ravjaa with a sword from his native land. No doubt this story has been exaggerated over the years and this one sounds like the opening scene of a Hollywood action film. Nonetheless, Gobi storytellers recall it with total conviction.

The sword received by Ravjaa is now on display in Sainshand along with other weapons including daggers and throwing stars. The handle of the saber contains the word "Morito." Some believe this was the name of the Japanese prince while others suggest it might be the name of an old Mongolian ethnic group. Still other guess it is connected to the Mongolian word *moir*, which means horse. Because of this, the Japanese student has been dubbed the "Horseman Hero."[105]

Another "travel story" begins with Ravjaa's entourage coming upon a lonely ger in the desert. When the ger owners learn that the great saint is nearby they invite him to enter so that he might say a prayer for their broken-hearted daughter. Ravjaa enters the ger and upon seeing the girl, promises that she will live. The girl then opens her eyes and, even though she had never before met Ravjaa, cries out that he is the man she has been waiting for. Her health is soon recovered and she is told by Danzan Ravjaa to learn a song called "Full Moon of the Month" (see chapter seven) which she practices to perfection. When Ravjaa later returns to the ger she impresses him so much with her voice that he invites her to join his drama company.[106]

Ravjaa's powers as a tantric practitioner played a large part in his mythological history. There are stories about his being able to fly, speak with the dead, disappear into thin air and turn water into vodka. Walking anywhere was hardly necessary when he could fly between distant points.

In one tale, a student of Ravjaa went on a pilgrimage to Wutai Shan (previously mentioned in chapter three). En route he stopped at a small monastery in Inner Mongolia in order to spend the night. While observing the activities of the monks, he noticed two lamas carrying dough sculptures out of the temple after the prayer session. The young Khamaryn Khiid monk exclaimed, "You take your sculptures outside using your own hands? At our monastery, the sculptures float outside by themselves!"

By saying this he was mocking his hosts, declaring that the lamas of Outer Mongolia, particularly those at Khamaryn Khiid, were more powerful than the monks of Inner Mongolia. Accepting this challenge the two monks said, "There is one sculpture left; please make it go outside by itself." Forced into the little temple with orders to sit before the remaining sculpture, the young monk suddenly found himself in a quagmire, for he had no power to move the statues. Nervously he sat before the altar and began to pray; but rather than pray for the sculpture to float out the door, he only prayed for Danzan Ravjaa's help. Over and over he whispered his teacher's name.

The lamas didn't notice he was calling for Ravjaa. Upon nightfall, the young monk opened his eyes and saw the sculpture float past his face and out the door. All the monks of the monastery, including the Hamba (Supreme) Lama, stood in amazement, and then bowed to the equally dumbfounded Outer Mongolian monk, who smiled shyly in their presence. The next day the young student quietly slipped out of the monastery and continued to Wutai, still overwhelmed by his accomplishment.

Upon his return home he met with Danzan Ravjaa, who smiled and asked, "Did you have a good journey? Did you see many interesting things?"

The young lama described his adventures in great detail, including the strange experience with the dough sculptures. Ravjaa laughed and said, "You were calling me all night and I could not sleep. So I went to help you. But you promised to do something you were not capable of doing on your own. You should only promise to do things that you can do!"[107]

Another popular story describing his 'super powers' tells that once, while traveling to Peking, Ravjaa met a beautiful child and gave her a book to read. The child's parents saw the man leave and when they entered the ger they asked their daughter who had given her the book. "Danzan Ravjaa!" she said with glee. The parents hurried outside to look for Ravjaa, but they couldn't see him. He had already traveled past the horizon. As a tantric practitioner, Ravjaa had the ability to travel great distances quickly; one of his footsteps could equal hundreds of normal steps.[108]

Other stories describe how Ravjaa used his power to save others. Once, after a heavy rain, a dry wash in the desert was swollen with floodwaters that swept away plants and livestock. One unfortunate herder was trapped in the torrent and called out to Danzan Ravjaa, pleading for help. The benevolent saint heard the man's cries and transformed himself into a large bush by the banks of the river so that the man could pull himself safely to shore. When he was at last safe, the man sat on the riverbank and complained bitterly, and with ironic humor, that a bush saved him instead of his lama.[109] It is these and many other stories that continue to fuel the high level of interest in Ravjaa, his poetry and the lore that surrounds him.

* * *

Ravjaa did not underestimate the value of friendship. When he was not locked up with his work he surrounded himself with companions, wrote about them, and waxed eloquent on how they are won and lost.

It was his belief that persons of high rank easily lose their companions because of their arrogant behavior. This is exemplified in one stanza from the poem, 'My Lama, Three Jewels':

All the birds flee from a dried-up pool
And friends of the Khaan flee from the hard of heart
Fruit and flowers flee from an infected tree
And close friends flee from those who are obstinate[110]

The lines confirm what we already know about Ravjaa; that he loathed arrogant behavior and recognized that disciples would desert any teacher who showed arrogance. Another poem, 'The Richness of Mount Semeru,' extols the virtues of friendship, its benefits and its obligations. Two stanzas of the poem are mentioned in the following:

> If you have a faithful companion,
> Even a darkened place can be musical.
> If you make friends in good faith,
> Joyful laughter is alluring.
>
> If you make friends in good faith,
> Where there is cruel mockery,
> You think of eternal friendship,
> And the day is long in passing.[111]

Historians and collectors of legend have pieced together the lives of several individuals associated with Danzan Ravjaa. One of the most prominently mentioned is Khilenhormoi, the *Sain Er* (good fellow) previously described as Ravjaa's bodyguard.

Khilenhormoi was one of many Sain Er or, as the Manchus called them, *magu qulagayici* (wicked robbers). The Sain Er, little more than brigands in today's terms, often made Chinese settlements the target of their raids. Most were army deserters who had little desire to defend the Chinese. The Sain Er were often ruthless in their attacks but were rarely organized. They traveled in small groups of five to six men, just enough for a highway robbery. They enjoyed special fame comparable to the likes of Jesse James or Robin Hood.

Togtaqu was probably the best known of all the Sain Er. An epic song about his career was still sung until the 1950s in Inner Mongolia. With the approval of Mongol banner authorities, he spent years antagonizing Chinese rule in Inner Mongolia. Between

1906 and 1910 he notched up no less than 104 raids against Chinese settlements, burning homes and tax records, stealing horses, gold, silver and other valuables, and distributing the booty to poor Mongol *arats*. Life was dangerous for such men. Chinese soldiers captured Togtaqu's wife and two of his children were killed in fighting, but he never turned himself in. Later in life, Togtaqu became the head bodyguard for the Bogd Gegeen in Huree, and served the Mongolian government until his death in 1922.[112]

Danzan Ravjaa's bodyguard, Khilenhormoi, lived a couple of generations before Togtaqu. He actually came from a high-ranking family. His father-in-law was a wealthy aristocrat and horse breeder named Dendev Taij. Khilenhormoi proved himself an honorable comrade on many shared trips with Ravjaa. He never felt hunger or cold and was compared to a wolf. He went to sleep late, got up early and frightened away potential bandits with his size and strength. But he was also fiercely independent and would disappear for days or weeks without warning.

Legend says that Khilenhormoi was arrested by Manchurian soldiers and charged with various criminal activities, including theft and murder. He was sent to Peking for trial (and, presumably, his death). While being escorted out of the Gobi, his caravan passed a group of Mongols traveling north. Khilenhormoi's arm was broken at the time – a horrible injury inflicted by his captors that had completely snapped the bone in two. According to the legend, he amputated his own arm, gave it to the travelers, and requested that it be sent to Ravjaa. The caravan men, still flabbergasted by the amputation, took the arm and delivered it to Danzan Ravjaa, who was 'pleased' to have a relic of his friend. The arm, dried and preserved, was used in religious ceremonies at Khamaryn Khiid for years to come. Before its ultimate destruction in 1937, Khamaryn

Khiid curator Tuduv reported seeing the arm still in an honored place of the monastery.[113]

Heissig tells a similar tale in his work *History of Mongolian Literature* Vol. 1. According to his research, Ravjaa befriended anyone who was anti-Manchu. In the Chahar area a man nicknamed the "Wild Black Hero" was imprisoned by the Manchus, his hands in irons and a yoke on his shoulders. This Wild Black Hero asked Ravjaa to do something, *anything*, to comfort him during this time of misery.

In response, Ravjaa gave the prisoner a mirror and a razor and said, "Be clear like a mirror and sharp like a razor." Although this might have been ironic or funny to Danzan Ravjaa, the Black Hero considered it auspicious and praised the monk. The objects in the end did little to help; the Wild Black Hero remained under the yoke until his death some 12 years later.

Another character mentioned earlier was the scientist Doyod, who helped Ravjaa select the location of Khamaryn Khiid. Doyod was a geographer and an expert in earth sciences. He was also a poet and described landforms and soil content in lyrical verse. Doyod's main responsibility was to consult with Ravjaa on where and how to build temples, based on ground structure and sources of water. He was an ultra-nationalist and gained the respect of his peers by constantly defying Manchu intervention into his work. He was also fond of making scientific hypotheses. He once told Ravjaa that far beneath the surface of the Gobi Desert there lay a great ocean. Even today, many Gobi people believe that their desert rests atop an ocean.[114]

One common theme running through Danzan Ravjaa stories is that he not only made friends easily, but he earned the respect of these friends through his extraordinary charisma.

Consider the friendship that Ravjaa developed with a famed shaman named Jambal. This native of Khövsgöl had come to Khamaryn Khiid with five other shamans to meet Danzan Ravjaa. Having heard that Ravjaa was himself a powerful magician, they challenged the monk to a competition and promised victory.

According to the legend, the five shamans conjured up a rainstorm with thunder and a fierce wind. Ravjaa only stood and watched, not bothered by the tempest swirling around him. The shamans did their best to defeat the hutagt but eventually collapsed from exhaustion. Ravjaa pretended as if nothing had happened at all. The shamans, having never seen such strength, immediately surrendered and bowed to Ravjaa. Jambal was so impressed that he decided to stay at Khamaryn Khiid to study with Ravjaa. Years later, upon his deathbed, Jambal promised that his spirit would "protect Khamaryn Khiid until every last brick disappeared." Following this remark, locals dedicated a hill near the monastery to Jambal, and still perform annual ceremonies to his spirit.

The list of heroes and villains is made complete with a nasty character named Us Getsul (Hairy Monk). This menacing personage was born in Inner Mongolia and spent several years in Tibet where he practiced black magic. He later settled at a place near Khamaryn Khiid called Gurvan Bayan.[115] His nickname was derived from his wild long hair, which supposedly supplied him with special powers. Us Getsul was famed for his knavery and ability to trick people out of their money; but he usually squandered his resources on gambling and women.

One story about Us Getsul describes how he met a Chinese trader in the desert and proposed a business deal. The trader was to give Us Getsul a large sum of silver in exchange for a flock of fat sheep with lovely wool coats. The trader agreed, handed over his silver coins and took his sheep, believing that he had struck a bargain. But that night the sheep vanished, leaving the trader with just some bits of wool. Us Getsul used his magic to steal the sheep back, which he sold time and again to unsuspecting traders.

Another legend tells about his theft of an animal stomach filled with oil. While en route to Tibet, Us Getsul stole one of these stomachs from a family he had stayed with. After fleeing the ger he continued on his way and came to a hill. But to his surprise and frustration he could not reach the top, being pulled back by some invisible force. The housewife from the ger, realizing her oil had been stolen, rode up to Us Getsul and said he could travel no further because a spell had been cast over him after he stole the stomach. She took back her oil, divided it in two, gave half to Us Getsul and sent him on his way.

Us Getsul traveled on to Tibet and became a powerful sorcerer, but never learned the lesson of kindness that the woman had taught him. Years later, upon his return to Mongolia, Us Getsul came upon the very same ger and wanted to test the black magic he had learned. He sat on the ground, stretched his hands out in front of him, closed his eyes and made an invocation for death. As he sat in the meditative state, he felt a hot bloody heart beating in his hands. At the last moment he 'returned' the heart to its owner.

Us Getsul, exhausted from his act of meditation, staggered into the nearby ger and saw the same woman who had given him the oil years before. Her face was pallid and covered in sweat. Her distressed husband stood above, holding her hand and wailing a prayer to the gods. "Please help us!" the old man cried. "My wife has nearly died!" Us Getsul stood silently, turned, and walked out the door. He had no remorse for his cruel deed.

It was under such circumstances that Ravjaa decided to punish his rival.

The incident began one day when Ravjaa suddenly, and without thinking, summoned his people to load up their camels with their belongings and travel into the desert. Ravjaa knew not why he was going, nor where, but only that he had to leave his monastery. Then, in mid-journey, Ravjaa stopped and realized that he was under a spell cast by Us Getsul. Furious with the prank, he started meditating, calling Us Getsul to his monastery.

The next day Us Getsul appeared with a basket of animal droppings on his back. He had been collecting *argols* when Ravjaa called, and under the spell hurried to Khamaryn Khiid without putting away his basket. When Us Getsul bowed before Ravjaa, the Fifth Hutagt cut off his long plait. The magician's face suddenly became ordinary because he had lost his powers. Thereafter, it is said, Us Getsul played no more tricks on the Gobi people.[116]

Danzan Ravjaa's scorpion seal

10

Travels and the Capital City

"Urga is the headquarters of the Buddhism of North Mongolia; it is also the stronghold of unblushing sin."[117] *James Gilmour, 1883*

Although mythology swirls around the middle years of Danzan Ravjaa's life – the friends he made, the foes he vanquished – the reality of his life was just as romantic as it had been in the days of heady travel and theatrical study that consumed his younger years.

As mentioned in chapter three, Ravjaa had spent much of his twenties in Inner Mongolia, studying theater in Chahar, Alasha and Doloon Nuur. In his early thirties, having dedicated himself to the staging of *Saran Khökhöö*, Ravjaa was found directing theater at Khamaryn Khiid and his monasteries in both Inner and Outer Mongolia.

It was at this time, with the production of *Saran Khökhöö* in full swing, that Ravjaa's worldview began to change. At the age of 31, in 1834, while traveling between Chahar and Peking, he wrote the poem 'Always True,' which includes lines such as:

Life has been tumultuous
I am sick of bearing life
While I am drunk with brandy
I don't have the strength
To sit in peace
So I say it in this grating poem

At this time, Ravjaa's addiction to alcohol seemed to be reaching a critical point, which may have been the reason for a slowing down in his activities in the mid-1830s. His biography passes over these years, only mentioning that in 1836 he traveled in southern Gobi Mergen Van and to Chahar to give Buddhist teachings.

The next significant event in Ravjaa's life occurred in 1839, when news came that the Bogd Gegeen had fallen gravely ill. Although much closer to the Janjiya Hutagt of Doloon Nuur, Ravjaa still felt honor-bound to assist Mongolia's spiritual leader and he immediately rushed to Huree to offer healing prayers for the Bogd.

Ravjaa then traveled west to Erdene Zuu Monastery at Karakorum, where he again prayed for the Bogd's good health. While in the area, Ravjaa studied the tsam mask traditions of Erdene Zuu and visited important sites including the hot springs at Hujirt and Tövkhön Monastery.

After wintering in the region, Ravjaa asked to return to Huree for another visit with the Bogd Gegeen, thus sparking one of the more curious incidents in his life.

*   *   *

By the 19th century, Huree had become a cosmopolitan city made up of Mongols, Chinese, Russians and Tibetan caravan men. The city had been founded around its temples but the times were changing in Huree and its importance as a spiritual center was compromised by the encroachment of a Han Chinese trading district called Maimaicheng. Life in the city was rough and foreign visitors generally lamented the degenerate state of affairs. Western accounts recall its packs of rabid dogs, its frequent outbreaks of disease, its abundance of brothels and the corpses deposited in its alleyways (which were eaten by dogs before they could rot). Even the monasteries themselves were impoverished. Many lamas were forced to become *dulduichin* (rattlers), roaming the streets offering their services as prayer readers and fortune-tellers.

Despite being welcomed to the city on previous visits, Ravjaa was refused entry on this final visit. He had apparently offended the Bogd on his previous visit by appearing drunk at his palace and refusing to remove his hat.

After being escorted out of the city, Ravjaa organized a feast at the Herlen River. It was here that Ravjaa wrote a song of forgiveness to the Bogd. The song, called 'Not to be Mocked,' was a hymn praising the Bogd as the 'Son of the World.' In the song he appeals to the Bogd not to mock him and promises to improve his behavior.

"Dumb to drink the brandy and trod in the way of the horses," Ravjaa said recalling his actions. "And then begged, you who are angry with me, he who spends his own dear life without being noticed, please forgive me."[118]

While camping by the Herlen River, Ravjaa was met by a number of local people who came for his blessing, including his lover Baljudmaa. Ravjaa wrote a love song for her called 'The Clever Brown One' (*Bardan Sergelen Borigoo*) in which he describes his sadness at seeing her go away, and his longing to join her in the great Khangai mountains.

> I want to train and ride
> My proud clever brown horse
> On my own will, trotting on the
> Highlands of the Khangai
>
> My only beloved
> Departing to distant places
> Yet as clear as a mirror
> Remains in my heart
>
> From the innermost parts of my body
> Missing You
> The glorious one
> Is like the spring inside a lock
>
> Let my wish come true
> Living together
> In the beautiful peaceful emptiness
> Of infinite space[119]

Ravjaa left the Herlen River and wintered in Hardal Beissin Hoshuu (Sükhbaatar Aimag), before traveling back to Doloon Nuur to visit with the Janjiya Hutagt. It was during this time that Ravjaa began to suffer from an ailment of the foot. His doctors said the ailment could not be healed and might be fatal. Grief-stricken, Dadishura then made five offerings in the hope of curing her companion. After a few weeks the ailment subsided and in gratitude, Ravjaa wrote 'Ulemchin Chanar' (chapter 7).

The coming year, 1841, Ravjaa announced his intentions to travel to Lhasa. He had never before been farther than Amdo, an area in the northern part of Tibet. By late February he had made it to Alasha, where he stayed to celebrate the lunar New Year. During the visit he watched various tsam performances and sacrificial rituals. It was here that an order came from the Janjiya Hutagt to return to his native country. Possibly because the incident came shortly after Ravjaa had been banned from traveling to Huree, he had fallen foul of the Gelugpa order, which may have prevented a trip to Lhasa. In any event, Ravjaa's biography mentions that, in appreciation of his visit, the people of Alasha gave him a gift of silver coins.

In 1843, Ravjaa traveled to his monastery in the southern Gobi, Gurvan Galbiin Khiid. He based himself here for several years, making only short trips and concentrating on the upkeep of his monasteries. In 1846, because of deteriorating health, Ravjaa made a trip to the natural spring area of Hujirt.

In 1853, the urge to travel struck Ravjaa again and he left to visit several monasteries across the Gobi. At Duinkhor Temple in Khamaryn Khiid he put on a tsam performance called 'The Way to Shambhala.' Traveling eastward, he stayed with the Hardal Beis in Tsetsen Khaan Aimag. It was here that he wrote a poem about the national Naadam celebration, which was carved into wood blocks for reprinting.

It was also in Tsetsen Khaan Aimag that Ravjaa is believed to have written 'Completely True Views,' now thought of as one of his last great works. The poem includes one of his signature remarks, "After with father and mother I became flesh and blood. I came with 18 years to this place. Then until today more than 40 years have passed, it really seems like magic to me."[120] Ravjaa concludes with the following ominous lines about traveling along the path to the underworld with the Hungry Ghosts.

> At the moment I travel to the Hungry Ghosts
> You my spiritual and worldly servants who stayed back
> Should live and do inner deeds that people will understand
> Because what I said earlier, harmonic vows and the teaching of the lama,
> These have gone away like a shadow in the evening
> Let us sing a drinking song together which pushes away the weariness
> For slowly I will follow the path and travel
> Difficult it is to go back, I hurry to go and to arrive
> And have sung a song for this path! [121]

In 1854 Ravjaa made one final journey to Huree, apparently to witness the enthronement of the seventh Bogd Gegeen.

This invitation and visit to Huree shows that Ravjaa, in his later years, had somehow made amends with the senior officials in Huree.

Following this trip to the capital, Ravjaa returned again to the desert by way of Erdene Zuu. The experiences he enjoyed on these trips, the poems he wrote, and the tsam performances he witnessed and directed, would be the last ones of his life.

11

An Untimely End

Oh, I am drunk
When the hour nears, you will die within a day and a
night
The body as soft as cotton and then as hard as wood
Your eyes clear as water and stiff as earth
Your belongings heaped up high as a rock
Will be covered with dust
The very dearest and closest friends turn into demons
Your serenity, burning like fire will collapse like ash
… Your fame like the wind will fade, like the rainbow
And one will throw away like an old fur
What you have treasured like gold[122]
Danzan Ravjaa

Danzan Ravjaa was still traveling and leading important Buddhist ceremonies until his death. His concise biography relates that in his final days, he was traveling south towards Inner Mongolia. He spoke with Dadishura, either on the road or at Khamaryn Khiid, and visited sacred sites and temples on the way. It is believed that his health was weak at this time, and he may have been heading to Inner Mongolia to pray for his own sake at the Maidari Temple (Maidar Juu or Meidai Zhao), a fortified monastery 70km west of Hohhot. Unfortunately for Ravjaa, the journey proved too long and he died en route. He was 53 years old. The year was 1856, coincidentally the same year in which the 11th Panchen Lama died.

A whole list of legend and lore provides various romantic versions of how Ravjaa met his end. The stories invariably place blame on one of his rivals, including the Manchus in Peking and the Gelugpa hierarchy in Huree. There were constant rumors that both intended to assassinate him. In order to thwart this, his followers provided a ring of security wherever he went. His libations were regularly tested for poison by pouring them into silver bowls. (If the drink were contaminated the cup would turn black). Visitors to Khamaryn Khiid were always viewed with suspicion and were sometimes searched for weapons or poison.

One legend states that, in 1853, Danzan Ravjaa gathered his disciples at a hill near Khamaryn Khiid and announced that he would "leave them" after three years. He ordered them to build an ovoo there and said they could always speak to him at this place, which he dubbed 'Shambhala,' the term used to define the mythical Buddhist kingdom. True to his word, Ravjaa passed away three years later. All the Mongolian versions of the death agree that he was poisoned, but few can agree as to who gave the poison, or why.

The historian Ts. Damdinsuren collected some of the more interesting versions of Ravjaa's death on his research trips to the Gobi Desert in the 1960s. These were later edited and updated by D. Tsagaan in her book *Ravjaagiin Yaruu Nairgiin Zokhioliin Toim*. The scholars guessed that Ravjaa's killers could have been the Gelugpa monks of Huree, a prince in Inner Mongolia, or even Dadishura. All could have been jealous of Ravjaa in some way. The most popular story involves the second wife of the Gobi Mergen Van, a practitioner of black magic named Shuluum Avai. (This combination of words loosely translates to 'Devil's Wife'). Because Ravjaa had long avoided her advances, Shuluum decided death was the best thing for him. Thus she gave seven bottles of vodka to a certain Luvson with instructions to deliver them as a gift to Ravjaa. One bottle contained poison. Luvson was given 50 lang to fulfill the mission. Ravjaa had "expected" a visitor to arrive "wearing a goatskin jacket and riding atop a black camel" and told his disciples to greet such a visitor warmly.

Days later, Luvson arrived in the exact manner that Ravjaa had predicted. "You merely took 50 lang from Shuluum Avai, but it is I that have known five lives. So is it you who should drink… or I?" Ravjaa asked when they finally met. Luvson was too afraid to answer. How could Ravjaa have known about the money? He began to wail with grief and then confessed to his crime.

"I will drink to fulfill the dreams of others," said Ravjaa. "Evil people have wealthy aims. This is the one law of the poor universe."[123]

Ravjaa did indeed drink the poison. If he knew that the vodka contained poison then he committed suicide, which is what many scholars believe.

After Ravjaa drank this poison he sat down to write his final poem, *Yertons Avgain Jam Khemekh Orshiv* (Law of the Universe Lady). This poem is a highly abstract and negative view of life – condemning and cursing the world as meaningless, dishonest and sinful; he further calls the world an evil monster capable of eating and killing.

The poem contains verses of emptiness, lamenting that the world is a dreamy void where death is inevitable, a place where the cries of the suffering are ignored. His words do not show anger, but rather an understanding of the nature of the world. The poem is his parting advice to his disciples that one should not seek happiness in the world. It reflects the Buddhist belief that only when a person can overcome suffering will they be able to follow the path to enlightenment. It reads in parts as follows:

Universe lady, to you
Let me give you simple jokes
To you with changeable manner
There is nothing interesting in you

You spiteful Universe lady
I am giving you one nickname
'Perfect pure vow Universe'
Who contradicted with the Buddha himself

Lazy sleeping world
Lost from power or strength of truth
You disturb all spirituality

Truly deceitful world
Which isn't there when one sees it
Crazily screaming world
Which fades while one listens

Prodigal and foolish world
Becomes wrong while you think of it

Uncompassionate gluttonous world
Not satisfied with what it has

Unwise sleeping world
Never waking
Unmerciful killing and eating
Most terrible monster world

Changeable in speed
Deceitful and slippery world
Completely naïve
Losing and wicked world

Being friends from the early ages
Disguised world
Earnestly urging without fail
Devil's leg world

Hiding your fault and being spiteful,
But having sickness in your abdomen.
Universal lady, to you
I will offer you simple jokes

Dear world, you think
You are nice?
I am drunk and I have free time
Let me present an interesting anecdote

Disagreeable Universe
For it's impossible to be disciplined

Universe burned with pride
For it's impossible to gain success

The world with attachment and passion
Never tired of tricking
Female unstable Universe you are
For you get upset when I say the truth[124]

The poem concludes, "I am hurt in this world, that I became a scoundrel. My poor father, these are the words of my sincere heart."

'Law of the Universe Lady' was supposedly written just after Danzan Ravjaa swallowed fatal poison, so one cannot guess the emotions coursing through his veins as he wrote these lines. Past critical works had been directed at different elements of society – lamas, aristocrats and others – rather than all-encompassing references to the world as a whole. Yet, on his deathbed, there was simply no single person worthy of his emotions, which were instead directed at the world itself.

In this poem, we see that Ravjaa chose to leave this world attached not to its beauty but to its worst qualities. It is in fact a very intimate poem as it shows a strong attachment, almost marriage, between the world and Ravjaa.

This relationship gave Ravjaa life, it led him through a difficult childhood, it killed his parents when he was young and it put him into constant conflict with authority. The world prematurely killed his predecessors and he predicted it would kill the Noyon Hutagts that would follow him. In the end, the world also took his life from him, as he expected it someday would.

*   *   *

Ravjaa's corpse was returned to Khamaryn Khiid and left in the hands of Balchinchoijoo, a high-ranking lama and man of noble blood. Balchinchoijoo swore an oath to protect the relics of Ravjaa, the words of which are still preserved on a wall hanging at the Danzan Ravjaa Museum in Sainshand: "Since Master Bogdo Chinggis Khaan became Heaven and bid farewell, his faithful Bo'orchu became the protector. Since beloved Noyon Hutagt became Heaven and bid farewell, I, Balchinchoijoo, became the protector of his temple."

Bo'orchu, as mentioned in the *Secret History of the Mongols*, was Chinggis Khaan's trusted assistant from a young age. When Chinggis died he took the role of caretaker for the great Khaan's most valued possessions. Balchinchoijoo likewise saw himself as the *takhilch* (protector, curator or trustee) for Ravjaa. The oath further affirmed three promises. The first, that items from Khamaryn Khiid were not personal property; they belonged to all Mongolians. The second promise held that the items could never leave Mongolia. The third promise affirmed that the takhilch was ultimately responsible for the objects.

Following Ravjaa's death, Balchinchoijoo's first task was to oversee the embalming and mummification of the monk – a rare funeral rite reserved for hutagts and other high incarnates. High lamas were commonly cremated. Their ashes were buried in holy sites or sometimes mixed with dough and turned into altar statues.

After a hutagt dies his body is left seated in the formal posture of meditation – legs crossed, right arm raised and holding a special item like a prayer bell or peacock feather. The body is then prepared for cremation; but when mummification is in order the embalming takes place the following day. First the skin is rubbed with perfume and oil. Then a compound containing salt, juniper and other preservatives is applied. The skin is then pricked with a needle to allow the preservatives to seep into the body. Following this, the entire corpse is covered with a mound of salt and left to dry for two months. The next step is to clean off the compound, dress the hutagt and decorate the face with gilt. The mummy, called a *sharil*, is then buried under a stupa or placed inside a temple where it can be worshipped.

Ravjaa's mummified body was placed inside his famous White Temple, which only Balchinchoijoo was permitted to enter. The White Temple became known as the 'mummy temple' and its doors were open to the public for a special viewing on just one day each year. Why would the lamas place Ravjaa in the White Temple, alongside 150 boxes filled with relics, artwork and books? It was said that local Manchu overlords sought to destroy Ravjaa's artifacts to erase his legacy. The clergy at Khamaryn Khiid, however, knew that even the Manchus would never destroy a tomb or grave; thus, placing the corpse in the same room with his belongings would protect both his body and his relics.

The responsibility of Danzan Ravjaa's takhilch was to be passed onto the descendants of Balchinchoijoo – whether they were monk or layman. Balchinchoijoo had a large birthmark on his back and it was said that future curators would bear a similar mark.

Balchinchoijoo died in 1865. However, his duties had already been taken over by his son Gan-Ochir (1837-1889), who assumed the role of takhilch at the age of 25. Gan-Ochir had been groomed for this position from a young age (having also been born with the auspicious birthmark) and spent his youth studying Danzan

Ravjaa's writings, poetry and teachings under the guidance of his father.

Naria, Gan-Ochir's son, assumed the role of the third curator. His son Ongoi served until 1931. However, it was actually Ongoi's brother Gombo who performed most of the curatorial duties at this time. Tuduv was the fifth curator until his death in 1990; his fate will be discussed in the next chapter. Each of these trustees underwent a similar education, each being taught by their father about the rich heritage of Danzan Ravjaa. Each studied Ravjaa's works and, importantly, the significance of the relics that he left behind. While little is known of their activities, it is believed that both Ongoi and Gombo played an important role in protecting Ravjaa's belongings during the chaotic era that followed the overthrow of the Manchu dynasty in 1911. At one point, with Kuomintang forces threatening monasteries in the Gobi, Ongoi and Gombo ordered an evacuation of the White Temple, successfully moving dozens of crates filled with relics into the Gobi Desert on the backs of camels.

During the time of these trustees, two more Noyon Hutagts were brought to Khamaryn Khiid, and both bore a tragic story. Following the death of Ravjaa, the Manchurians proclaimed that all future Noyon Hutagts must be found in Tibet. This was a common practice used to undermine their power. The same law had applied to the Bogd Gegeens, after the second Bogd (a Mongolian) had attempted to lead a revolt against the Manchus. After that, all Bogd Gegeens were brought from Tibet to weaken alliances and create friction within the Mongolian hierarchy.

The sixth Noyon Hutagt was named Luvson Dambi Jantzen Odser. He was born in Tibet and grew up within the Gelugpa yellow hat tradition. He was actually the younger brother of the seventh Bogd Gegeen. So illegitimate was this 'reincarnation' that he was actually born a year before Danzan Ravjaa died. He was taken to Peking for further schooling and Manchu indoctrination, to be used as a puppet in the Gobi. At the age of 14, he was sent to Khamaryn Khiid with 60 Tibetan families.

Things went poorly from the start. The monks considered the boy an unworthy leader, mainly because he was Tibetan, not a Mongol. He received a poor education and it is likely that he was beaten. In return, the sixth hutagt condemned his predecessor and ordered the destruction of his artwork and literature. This, clearly, did not sit well with Ravjaa's friends and disciples. He managed six years at Khamaryn Khiid before he was poisoned.

"After that the people chose a *real* Hutagt," the current curator Altangerel explained.

Following the assassination of the young Tibetan, negotiations were carried out to allow the seventh Noyon Hutagt to be born in Mongolia. It is unclear, however, how long this process took and when precisely the seventh Hutagt was born. Historians write that he was born in 1875 or 1876. However, other evidence suggests he was not born until 1891. This is based on an official document from 1931 stating that the seventh Hutagt was 40 years old at that time. (It is possible that this document was mistaken). Whatever the year of his birth, the fact that he was allowed to assume the role of the seventh hutagt was important for the morale of the people in Gobi Mergen Van Khoshuu. His mother was Tserendejid (nicknamed Jinje) and he allegedly had very clear signs of being a hutagt. At his ordination, he was granted the name Agvan Luvson Dambi Jantzen Jampts.

Like Danzan Ravjaa, the Seventh Hutagt enjoyed widespread popularity and was well traveled. He visited both Peking and

Huree. Legend has it that he also went to Lhasa and India, although this is probably untrue. He was known for putting on great feasts, punctuated with heavy bouts of drinking, and for promoting horse racing and the arts.

The Seventh Hutagt also revived Ravjaa's theater. He personally directed springtime performances of *Life Story of the Moon Cuckoo*. In order to raise funds for the play he even set up a financial department at Khamaryn Khiid, which collected money for the opera.

To improve the skills of his actors he pumped money into the drama school set up by the Fifth Hutagt. The drama company had, however, fallen off somewhat from Danzan Ravjaa's day. For one, the length of the opera was shortened from one month to around two weeks, ending the story at the time of Nomun-Bayasgalant's birth. The Seventh Hutagt halved the number of actors, musicians and crew. While not as prolific as Danzan Ravjaa, the Gobi people were convinced of his status as the true Gobi Noyon Hutagt.

Legends about the Seventh are few but I managed to uncover one story related to his life, perhaps based on factual accounts. It was said that in the year 1910 there lived in the Gobi an insane brother and sister, the children of a certain Ja Getsul. The pair acted strangely when visitors came to their ger, often stripping down to their undergarments and fondling each other. Their family members knew this and tied them up. Nevertheless, this was one ger rarely visited by neighbors.

One time the seventh Noyon Hutagt came to the ger. When the insane siblings saw him they were overcome with such fright that they ran away into the desert and died soon afterwards. Gobi people believe that the brother and sister were in fact reincarnations of Luvson and Shuluum Avai and that they were born insane as "payment" for killing Danzan Ravjaa. This was why they had so feared the seventh incarnation.[125]

*   *   *

Mongolia's embrace of Stalinism in the 1930s spelled doom not only for the Seventh Hutagt but also for Buddhists across the country. Life grew so bad in the monasteries that many monks were forced to flee across the borders into China, Tuva and Russia. Few fared any better in these similarly unstable countries.

Khamaryn Khiid was unable to escape the chaos that engulfed the country. Shortly after the arrival of communism, livestock belonging to the monastery was confiscated and the monks saw their religious activities restricted. In 1931, scores of lamas from Khamaryn Khiid were arrested for 'counter-revolutionary activities' and taken to Ulaanbaatar (Huree). Their fate is not known but it is likely that they were either executed or died in labor camps. Among those arrested was the curator Ongoi and the 40-year-old seventh Noyon Hutagt. The monastery was closed temporarily and the remaining monks, including Ongoi's son Tuduv, were scattered about the region.

The official responsible for the Hutagt's arrest was named Luvson, coincidentally sharing his name with Danzan Ravjaa's killer. Luvson, a captain in the army, ordered the immediate removal of the Seventh Hutagt's property. His investigation was well documented in a series of reports which ran in parts as follows:

"I thought they (the Seventh Hutagt and an aristocrat named Baljinyam) were very strange. But they knew what they were doing. They secretly divided their possessions to their followers, who hid their treasure and distributed their livestock. Because of our work, the people did not like our office. They said we are slaves and beggars to the government. Some people cursed the officials, others feigned suicide, some tried blackmail and bribes. Still others said they would seek revenge. But the Seventh Hutagt and Baljinyam were not such people, they were very calm.

"The Seventh Hutagt was 40 years old. He was fat and yellow and had a big red nose. He owned a big cup for *arkhi* and drunk this alcohol like a thirsty camel drinks water. He was also addicted to snuff. He would fill the palm of his hand with this snuff and all at once sniffed it into his nose; some fell onto his chest causing his clothes to be constantly dirty. He had no close relatives at all, except two adopted daughters.

"When we met him we announced that we would take his property, and he did not protest, saying he knew of this before. 'Good deeds and sin, happiness and suffering all have their time. Now the time changes for me. I have some property but I don't know where it all is, you should meet our lamas who are officially responsible for this. Perhaps others can benefit from this property. I have two adopted daughters and you can decide what to leave them. I only request that you leave me my vodka and tobacco,' the Hutagt said.

"After we collected the Hutagt's livestock along with his precious artifacts a district official said that many more valuables were hidden in the ground. We accused the Hutagt of this and interrogated him about the whereabouts of the property.

"He said, 'I hid nothing, and as I told you I do not know how much property I have nor where it is. My financial manager Mishig knows this and I think he has created this conflict. You should interrogate him. I actually do not oppose your government; people know that every year I willingly gave 40 horses to the army in Zamyn Uud, now I want to leave the monastery and join the army.'

"Then, as before, he asked in a friendly tone, 'My son, I have no regrets about my property, but I regret that I don't have my *arkhi*.' And he asked me to bring him some. I reported this conversation to the district head and he allowed me to give one kettle of vodka from the Hutagt's supply. The Hutagt drank the entire kettle and then laid down in a very happy state.

"He then said, 'If I hid any property I would tell you, but I didn't hide anything so please talk to Mishig.' Then he asked for more *arkhi*. I returned the next day and gave him two kettles, and on the third day I gave three as the district head allowed. This official said if we didn't give the Hutagt *arkhi* he would die there. I had never seen any person whose life was sustained by alcohol. I had never met such a person before or after.

"The Hutagt spent ten days in prison and was then taken to Ulaanbaatar via Hentii. Because of his great girth, he was unable to ride a horse, so he was taken on a cart. After he left we interrogated Mishig, who confessed that he and others had hidden the Hutagt's gold and silver.

"The Fifth Hutagt was a drunk, and this is why he was given names such as the 'Crazy Noyon Hutagt' and the 'Horrible Saint.' He grew infamous by these names. I have heard the legends told by local people about how the Fifth Hutagt predicted that the Sixth would live for a short time and that the Seventh would be like himself, a drunkard. The legend says that there will be no more Noyon Hutagts after the Seventh is gone. We all know that the Fifth Hutagt was a famous man of culture and a great poet. We still sing the songs he composed and know of the drama 'Saran Khökhöö' which he directed.

"I doubt that the Noyon Hutagt could predict the life of his reincarnations. But in any case, I have seen that the seventh incarnation was a drunk with no bounds."[126]

It's likely that the Seventh Hutagt was shot dead and buried in a mass grave on the outskirts of Ulaanbaatar, as was the fate of many monks at the time. According to a new law, the recognition of a hutagt was not permitted. While the Gobi people had heard this before, the proclamation this time was coming not from Peking but from the Mongolian capital Ulaanbaatar.

The incarnations of Yansang Yidam that had spanned hundreds of years had come to an abrupt end.

It is interesting to note that five Noyon Hutagts in a row were either murdered or committed suicide. The Third and Fourth were executed by the Manchus in Peking, the Fifth seems to have committed suicide, the Sixth was assassinated by the Khamaryn Khiid lamas and the Seventh by the Mongolian Communists. It was by no means a golden era.

Even though history records that the line ended with the Seventh Hutagt, there was in fact a secret Eighth Noyon Hutagt.

The story begins in 1930 when hundreds of Mongolians were fleeing Mongolia to escape Communist repression. Among them was Gendensaivan, assistant to the Seventh Noyon Hutagt (and great-uncle of the museum curator Altangerel). While at Shilingol (Inner Mongolia), Gendensaivan learned that the Seventh Hutagt had been arrested and was presumed dead. He took it upon himself to find a reincarnation. After much searching and interviewing, Gendensaivan identified a possible reincarnate, a young boy who went by the name of Samdan Jampts. He selected this child because it was said that the baby cried for three days after his birth. He refused to drink milk and only stopped crying when his mother offered a taste of vodka. The baby drank it, and was recognized as a reincarnation of a "drunk hutagt." However, because of the political situation in Mongolia, the boy and Gendensaivan remained in Shilingol. Today, Outer Mongolians do not consider Samdan Jampts to be a bona fide Hutagt because he never received ordination at Khamaryn Khiid.

Continuing the trend of premature deaths, the Eighth Hutagt died at the age of 12, a casualty of war. It is said that he was killed while his monastery was being ransacked towards the end of WWII.[127]

* * *

A year after the arrest of the Seventh Noyon Hutagt, northern Mongolia erupted into a civil war between the monasteries and the Communist government. It was a short but bloody campaign that saw great losses on both sides. After a brief period of peace, violence erupted again in 1937 with the Great Purge, ending in the deaths of around 28,000 monks and the destruction of hundreds of monasteries. By the end of 1938, there was little left of Mongolia's great Buddhist heritage.

As described in the report by the army captain Luvson, Khamaryn Khiid was closed in 1931. Many of the resident monks were taken away and the Seventh Hutagt was arrested and not heard from again. Luvson's report also indicates that the lamas and local people managed to hide much of the property belonging to the monastery. The Seventh Hutagt stated that one of his clerks, a certain Mishig, was responsible for the items. As it is understood today, the person actually responsible for the relics was Ongoi, Altangerel's great-grandfather. When the Seventh Hutagt said that "Mishig" was responsible he may have been trying to throw the officials off track, diverting their attention away from Ongoi and other monks involved with the protection of his relics. Because Ongoi was arrested along with the other monks in 1931, the role of curator fell on the shoulders of Tuduv, Ongoi's son.

One of the final decisions the lamas made prior to their arrest was what to do with Danzan Ravjaa's mummified body. Still sealed up in its honored place inside the White Temple, the monks knew full well that it would soon be desecrated. Some wanted to bury it, but at last it was decided that the mummy should be burned. The ashes and bone fragments were saved by Tuduv and are now on display in the Danzan Ravjaa Museum.

Although the monastery was effectively closed in 1931, the temples were not destroyed until 1937. In fact, the monastery briefly re-opened for a time and some monks resumed their normal lives of prayer. The government kept a watchful eye on the monastery during this period. But in 1937, when Communist leader Choibalsan launched his "final solution", the monastery was obliterated. It was during this year that Tuduv managed to hide many of the treasure-filled crates in the desert. As for the monastery, usable parts were moved out of the area and stone blocks were used to make new buildings in the nearby town of Orgon. Some were used to construct an auto garage in Sainshand, and a few found their way to the town square where they were fitted into the ground in front of the Mongolian People's Revolutionary Party headquarters, where they still lie today.

Tuduv barely managed to escape the carnage at Khamaryn Khiid. He ran off into the desert until he reached the ger of his sister, where he remained to begin a new life as a herder. The years went by and Tuduv married a local girl. Together they raised a daughter and an adopted son. Tuduv did not tell his family about the boxes he had buried. Instead he simply prayed to himself that the restrictions on Buddhism would end and he could one day help to rebuild the monastery. As for Danzan Ravjaa, his name and all he had worked for had essentially vanished.

12

Ravjaa Resurrected

In the late 1950s, purely by chance, there was a renewed interest in the story of the forgotten monk. It was Ts. Damdinsuren, a well-known scholar, writer and professor of history and literature at Mongolian National University, who took an interest in Danzan Ravjaa.

Damdinsuren's adventure began in 1959 when he was leafing through some old textbooks at Gandan Monastery, the only Buddhist sanctuary left open under the Communist regime. He had only come by chance, as he was guiding some foreign tourists around the grounds.

While in the monastery library, he stumbled across ten volumes of *The Life Story of the Moon Cuckoo*. Some of the volumes were doubles and chapters one, three and five were missing, so the text was far from complete.

Damdinsuren's discovery was actually nothing out of the ordinary; many copies of this old Tibetan play existed. Sayabadar, a herder from the Gobi Desert, had brought these volumes to Gandan Monastery where a clerk filed them away. But after reading a few pages of the text Damdinsuren realized this manuscript was unique. The text included stage directions as though it were a script for a play or opera. Another volume, dated '1902,' was also located but this was filled solely with stage directions. This was not the Inner Mongolian or Tibetan version Damdinsuren had seen before. It was a fragment of Danzan Ravjaa's own play.

At that time, it was not known if Danzan Ravjaa had ever put on a performance, so effective had the Communist government been in erasing his legacy. There had been many rumors but no proof had been found until Damdinsuren's discovery.

Spurred on by this find, Damdinsuren became obsessed with learning more about the Fifth Hutagt, a historical figure his colleagues had dubbed "the drunken God of the Gobi Desert."

Damdinsuren became the pre-eminent researcher on the subject, writing about Ravjaa's mysterious and unique lifestyle. In 1961, after much research, he wrote down 20 of Danzan Ravjaa's songs that had only been recorded orally.

As for understanding the history of Danzan Ravjaa himself, Damdinsuren used a copy of the biography that had been found in 1952. It was believed that this text had been based on an autobiography, since it often speaks in the first person. He published a new biography on Ravjaa's life in 1962 and his lectures and reports soon changed the way in which Communist ideologues viewed the monk. Ravjaa was no longer considered a feudal relic, but now a great writer and social critic.

Damdinsuren began conducting interviews with elderly scholars and lamas and learned that *The Life Story of the Moon Cuckoo* had been widely performed in different Mongolian monasteries even long after Ravjaa's death. One 67-year-old former monk named Renchindorj said he had seen *Saran Khökhöö* twice when he was 18 or 19 in the area of present day Dornogobi, which would have been around the year 1911.

In April 1960 the Mongolian Academy of Sciences lent Damdinsuren a Russian Jeep Gaz-69 so that he could conduct research in Sainshand, Khövsgöl sum and other places associated with Ravjaa's life. His mission was to find the missing volumes of the opera. On the way he met former monks who said they had seen it performed when they were young. There was even a rumor that a famous *Life Story of the Moon Cuckoo* actress was still alive somewhere in northern Mongolia. Some of those interviewed were able to describe the costumes, the plot of the play, some of the action and perhaps recite a few lines of a song from the opera.

Finding the missing volumes of *Saran Khökhöö* proved to be one of the most challenging parts of his research. "It was like searching for a pearl in a field," he wrote.

On several occasions Damdinsuren was led to remote parts of the desert, based on advice or tips he had received from colleagues. There, they said, he would find an old person who had in his possession copies of the play. The information was often misleading; Damdinsuren spent days searching for herders who, when he met them, reported not having any lost manuscripts.

At last he met Damdarjaa, a worker at an oil well in Zuunbayan sum, who had a copy of the third volume. Soon after, he met a school teacher named Zanabazar who offered him a special edition of the second volume. This volume contained the lines of just two characters, and appeared to be a script for the opera.

Damdinsuren then came across the mother of all finds when he met an old blacksmith named Balbar, nicknamed Buduun (Fat) Baval, who lived southwest of the oilfield. Balbar was able to produce the first, third and fifth volumes of *The Life Story of the Moon Cuckoo*. So happy was Damdinsuren at having finally collected the whole opera, and so impressed was he with Balbar, that the professor took the time to pen his own poem dedicated to the blacksmith. It reads as follows:

I heard about the great poet
I started the journey to find his poems
Across the oasis
I went further
I arrived at the home of Balbar the blacksmith
And I stayed there

Balbar the blacksmith
I saw him using his hammer
Then he opened his special box
He removed from it carefully wrapped books

Among the books I found the poems I sought
I found the Noyon Hutagt's literature works
I admire the peaceful blacksmith
Who had that special box full of books
In his ten strong fingers

There is knowledge in the harsh Gobi
There is wisdom in the old man
There are books in the special box
These should not be neglected

The difficulties in conducting this research are described in Damdinsuren's book *Mongoliin Uran Zokhioliin Ov Ulamjaliin Asuudaluud* (Problems of Traditional Heritage in Mongolian Literature). The story explains how in the course of his journey, he heard about a certain Agvanzundui, who apparently had a part of the *Saran Khökhöö* play. After searching for some time it became clear that Agvanzundui had died, but just before his death he had buried his cache of Buddhist treasures in the desert. Further questioning proved that a girl called Tsetseg had helped to bury the chests. Damdinsuren succeeded in locating Tsetseg and she agreed to help find the chests. Damdinsuren then borrowed a Jeep from the director of the nearby oil drilling station (he doesn't say what had happened to his own Jeep) and organized a team to hunt for the chests.

The team included the school teacher Zanabazar, three students, a railway worker named Gombo, Tsetseg and four others, all crammed into the five-seat Jeep. Following the instructions of Tsetseg, the team set out for a place called Shar Dov, where the boxes would be found in a three or four square meter spot, "between two bushes."

"We left at 3pm and drove 70 kilometers through sand," Damdinsuren wrote. "We arrived at Shar Dov and started digging, but since we only had a couple of shovels we worked in five-minute shifts. We dug until 9pm and a nearby herder named Shorhon gave us food. The next morning we started digging at 6am and worked until 9pm. Of course it was exhausting. We dug six feet into the ground, the area was about the size of a ger, but we found nothing. This was very discouraging, so we stopped."

Later in the spring, Damdinsuren writes, Zanabazar took it upon himself to return to the site, this time with a local elder. "The old man had an iron rod and he hit the ground with it. If the earth was very hard he knew it had not been disturbed. But if it was soft he said that the boxes might have been buried on that spot. So they searched in this way and found two boxes. This old man was uneducated but wise because of the experiences life had given him. He had the wisdom of ten men," Damdinsuren wrote. Although the boxes did contain important Buddhist relics and books, they did not contain any volumes of *Saran Khökhöö*.

Although Damdinsuren had already published the events of this field trip, this did not stop others from conjuring up their own version of the adventure. J. Zundui was one of the three students on the expedition; he recorded his thoughts in 2003 for a newspaper to promote the 200th anniversary of Danzan Ravjaa's birth. He was 14 at the time and said the expedition occurred in July 1957 (Damdinsuren recorded the date as April 1960). Despite this, he said he had met Damdinsuren while he was in the process of interviewing some of the elders.

"Most of them were very scared and didn't talk too much, so Damdinsuren greeted them with a silk *khadak* and 25 tögrögs, which was a lot at that time," Zundui recalled. "Then we heard about an old man who had buried some boxes in the ground. We found his granddaughter who had helped him. She said she was 38 years old. She took us to the place where she thought the boxes were buried, we set up three gers for our own use, and we started to dig. However, it was very sandy and it seemed that whatever we dug up just fell right back into the hole. This digging went on for five days, and then on the sixth day a local family told us about an old temple that was 20 kilometers away. We found the ruins of this old temple and decided to dig there; it was a nice place with bushes and water. We dug about two meters into the ground and found a blue silk scarf. Then we found three boxes wrapped up in a *khadak*, it was very exciting. The next morning we laid out some cloth and opened these finely painted boxes; there we found the third, fourth, fifth and sixth volumes of the play that Damdinsuren was looking for. Damdinsuren was so happy, he was holding the boxes and jumping up and down."[128]

We can probably assume that Damdinsuren's version was more accurate. In either case, the professor's mission was complete; he had collected all the volumes of *Saran Khökhöö*, several poems and many stories about Danzan Ravjaa. Damdinsuren launched his mission to popularize Danzan Ravjaa and in 1961 published an article on the poet in *Culture and Literature* newspaper.

In 1962 Damdinsuren published a book containing Danzan Ravjaa's *The Life Story of the Moon Cuckoo* along with detailed notes on its stage direction. He and his pupil D. Tsagaan then set about editing the many poems they had converted into the Cyrillic script. By 1968 they had published 170 different poems, songs and *surgaals* that were originally written in Mongolian script and 180 pieces originally written in Tibetan script. They continued to piece together Danzan Ravjaa's biography, which was no easy task, since at least three versions existed. One copy had been brought to Gandan Monastery in 1959 by an anonymous man and given to Jambal, a lama in residence there. A second copy had been in the possession of the lama Gombo from Sainshand and a third had been held by the previously mentioned blacksmith Balbar.

Another problem Damdinsuren and Tsagaan continually faced was determining the original language of the poetry, as Danzan Ravjaa wrote in both Tibetan and Mongol. 'Shame and Shame,' 'Perfect Quality' and 'The Kite' were some of the poems for which the researchers could not determine the original language. They also found that Ravjaa had transliterated some of his Mongolian poems into Tibetan script so Tibetans could read the words even if they could not understand them.

*   *   *

During this time Lama Tuduv must surely have heard about Damdinsuren's investigations, but showed amazing resilience in maintaining his secret. As early as 1960 Damdinsuren mentioned having known that Tuduv was one of the old monks who might have information about Danzan Ravjaa, but Tuduv managed to avoid meeting with the professor. He believed secrecy was the best way to protect the hidden boxes.

Lama Tuduv had a wife, a daughter and an adopted son but he had said nothing to them with regard to the treasure-filled chests. The secret was his alone but he hoped the Communist storm would soon pass and that the secret could be revealed. However, as the years went by the situation remained unchanged, and Tuduv worried that he would have no heir to carry on the tradition of the takhilch. A fortuitous event then occurred.

Tuduv's daughter and her husband were at this time living in Ulaanbaatar. The daughter gave birth to a boy at Ulaanbaatar's Maternity Ward #2 and named him Altangerel (he would be the third of ten children). The mother noticed a large birthmark on the back of her newborn child and knew that her father bore a similar mark. She saw this as an auspicious sign and immediately contacted Dornogobi Province to alert her father of the arrival of her son and his unique birthmark.

When Tuduv heard the news he traveled straight away to Ulaanbaatar and the maternity ward where his daughter and grandson were recuperating. Having inspected the birthmark on the baby boy, Tuduv believed that this child could be groomed to one day replace him as takhilch. Explaining to his daughter that he wanted a child to keep him company he asked that when the boy was old enough he be sent to stay with him in the Gobi.

When Altangerel was still a small child, Tuduv took him to the Gobi and raised him according to the prescribed traditions of the takhilch. However, since Khamaryn Khiid no longer existed and Buddhism was banned under the law, Altangerel's education would be made in secret. He would not have the benefit of openly studying Ravjaa's works or researching the relics left behind in the "White Temple." Everything he would learn would be passed by word of mouth from his grandfather Tuduv.

When Altangerel was old enough, Tuduv took him out to the desert to describe the location of the chests that he had buried. There were 64 crates in 17 different locations and Altangerel was forced to memorize them all. If he forgot, Tuduv showed him a way to locate the boxes by using the light from the full moon on the 15th day of the middle month of the lunar year. Over the years, Tuduv and Altangerel opened each box to study their contents. Altangerel had to memorize the details of each item and recite them back to his grandfather.

Each of the 17 locations contained three or four boxes. Tuduv and Altangerel dedicated at least one week to the process of excavation, research and re-burial of the crates. Some of the items were brought back to their ger so that Altangerel could study them at night. Other herders in the area knew that Tuduv was privately training Altangerel to be a lama, although they knew nothing of the secret crates.

As the crates were re-packaged, Tuduv showed Altangerel

traditional methods of preservation. Metal items, for example, were smeared with horse fat to prevent corrosion. Tuduv even went to the extreme measure of breaking down the crates themselves so that the wood slats could be boiled in horse fat, thus ensuring their longevity. When the boxes were put back together, a sack of dung ash was left at the bottom and top of the crate to absorb moisture. Each crate was then placed in a leather sack; the seams were sealed with a mixture of resin and ash. Just before the last opening was sewn shut, a flame was placed inside the sack to displace the oxygen. When the crate was entombed, wood poles were placed around it in the shape of a teepee, forming a protective barrier against moisture that might seep through the earth.

Tuduv regaled Altangerel with the myths and legends of Danzan Ravjaa and forced his grandson to recite long passages of text written by Ravjaa. He brought six former lamas to visit them and help Ravjaa understand Buddhist philosophy, meditation and yoga. Tuduv also instructed Altangerel how to read and write in both Tibetan and the traditional Mongol script (which had been phased out by the government in the 1930s–1950s), so that he could properly study Ravjaa's works if the boxes were ever uncovered.

"Tuduv brought Altangerel very close. He taught him the things he needed to know and most importantly how to keep his word. It was not a normal relationship between grandfather and grandchild, it was one of teacher and student," said Danzan Ravjaa scholar and Altangerel's long-time colleague G. Tsagaanderem.[129]

Otgonasan, a relative of Altangerel, described how his own family was suspicious of Tuduv's family. "They were very strange, they never moved their ger. When the other herders were moving around in search of better grassland they just stayed in the same place. In 1990 we learned why they acted in this way – they were just staying near all those buried boxes. They kept their secret and protected Danzan Ravjaa's belongings, but at the time it was very unusual,"[130] Otgonasan said.

Altangerel will be the first to admit that he did not have an ordinary childhood. As a non-person for most of his youth, Altangerel grew up in a cocoon of religion and history.

"I was a hidden child. If someone came to our ger I had to stay in the storage tent until they left. I was very quiet even into adulthood. I didn't talk to anyone. My grandfather taught me how to meditate and control my emotions."[131]

Altangerel remembers his grandfather as a strict disciplinarian who filled his childhood with studies, hardship and labor. Altangerel was required to wake up early each morning to recite prayers. After his chores of collecting dung, cleaning the ger and preparing the fire, Altangerel was allowed breakfast, which consisted of one cup of tea and one biscuit. For lunch he was granted one bowl of rice and for dinner one bowl of meat. When he was seven, Altangerel was allowed to attend boarding school in Sainshand where he was given more food, but in summer he returned to his grandfather's ger and the hated food rations.

As an example of Tuduv's demeanor, Altangerel recalls one incident that occurred during his teenage years.

Tuduv had run into some trouble with the law after performing illegal Buddhist rituals. He was arrested and ordered to spend three days in the local prison in Sainshand. When Altangerel learned of this he was overjoyed at being allowed time away from his grandfather and celebrated by eating a month's supply of food. Tuduv beat him severely when he returned from prison.

Such a beating, however, was not uncommon. Tuduv beat

his grandson for the slightest offense and forced him to perform cruel tasks such as carrying a sack of sharp stones on his bare back over long distances. For further punishment, Tuduv forced his grandson to sleep in a cemetery, a taboo place for Mongolians and a frightening experience for any child. Altangerel now believes that there was a reason for this hardship. He states that Tuduv challenged him as preparation for the trials of life and the difficulties that would come with being a bona fide takhilch.

Tuduv and Altangerel suffered one major setback during those years. In 1969 a herder grazing his cattle found some of the crates that had been hidden in a cave. When the herder reported the find to the authorities, policemen and officials were deployed to investigate the site. Several crates filled with priceless relics were unearthed and burned in a great pyre. Young Altangerel and his grandfather watched all of this from a distance, careful not to interfere.

"If we had protested, we would have been arrested and interrogated. They could have forced us to give up all the boxes. There were already rumors that our family was hiding a cache of Buddhist objects, so we didn't want to make the situation worse,"[132] said Altangerel.

Because Tuduv had the relics catalogued, he knew what was lost; the cache included manuscripts, dels, hats and masks and some stage decorations, including a fake tree and horse. How odd it must have been for the officials to dig up theater props from the Gobi sands; and how heartbreaking it must have been for Altangerel and Tuduv to watch it go up in flames.

Altangerel began his compulsory military service at the age of 20. He arranged it so that he would be stationed in Sainshand and was assigned as a truck driver, which allowed him some opportunities to secretly meet with his grandfather. In 1984, Tuduv was ready to pass the torch of takhilch to his grandson. Together they rode horses into the Khar Uul Mountains and there Tuduv made Altangerel swear an oath to protect the legacy of Danzan Ravjaa, just as he had done at the age of 24. A special snuff bottle was passed from grandfather to grandson, marking the auspicious occasion. At that moment, Altangerel recalls, his grandfather apologized for having made his life so difficult, explaining that such methods were necessary to prepare him for the challenges ahead. Tuduv told him to keep the boxes safe until better times. He also advised Altangerel to train his own son to become a takhilch.

One year later, Altangerel left the army and began coursework at the Ulaanbaatar Pedagogical Institute, where he trained to be a history teacher.[133]

*   *   *

Meanwhile, Damdinsuren kept hot on the trail of Danzan Ravjaa from a more academic standpoint. He and Tuduv first met in 1976, but no mention of the crates was made for another nine years. By 1985 Damdinsuren was frail and near the end of his life. Because of this, and coupled with the fact that Mongolia was showing signs of liberalization, Tuduv at last revealed his secret. The old historian was overjoyed and wanted to travel to Dornogobi to uncover the crates, but his age would not allow another desert expedition. Instead Damdinsuren dispatched his long-time student, D. Tsagaan. Together, Tuduv, Altangerel, Tsagaan and Tsagaan's husband went back to Sainshand and secretly uncovered some of the boxes. They inspected some of the items but made no public mention of the artifacts.

In 1988, Tuduv decided the time had come to reveal something of his past. He was quoted in a newspaper article as saying that some of Danzan Ravjaa's relics could be found in the Gobi, and that his grandson would be responsible for them. The revelation shocked Altangerel, who worried that the news might get him into trouble with the authorities, but the matter passed without incident. Later that year, a group of artists met at a newspaper office in Sainshand and discussed how the legacy of Danzan Ravjaa could be restored. Altangerel attended the meeting and agreed to pursue his study of Danzan Ravjaa, but still said nothing of the hidden crates.

Tuduv died on December 9, 1990, the very same year that freedom of religion was restored in Mongolia. But his mission was complete; he had preserved the relics of Danzan Ravjaa.

Over the following months, Altangerel, Tsagaan and some of their friends from Sainshand exhumed half of the 64 original crates. More than 50 years after being buried in the sand, Ravjaa's belongings were again available for all to inspect and study. The materials from the crates were studied, analyzed and filed. Much of it was undertaken on an ad hoc basis, with various relics lying in heaps inside Altangerel's home.

G. Tsagaanderem, a colleague of Altangerel, explains the elation felt by those that helped to recover the crates. "We drove into the desert and Altangerel pointed to a place where we could find one of the boxes. We dug into the ground, found the crate and took it to a winter stable. We opened it there and took out some garments and costumes. There were some statues, metal and brass objects. We cleaned the dust off and let the fresh air settle into the box. The artifacts were amazing; I had never seen anything like them. Even the museums didn't have such things. No one had seen objects like these since the 1930s."[134]

More Danzan Ravjaa paraphernalia started popping up in

unforeseen places. One of the most significant objects recovered was an important image of Padmasambhava measuring about 16 inches tall. For years after the 1931 sacking of Khamaryn Khiid this silver statue had been kept hidden by a former lama in Sainshand, until it was stolen from his home in 1970. Somehow the relic was sold again and ended up in the treasury of Mongol Bank in Ulaanbaatar. There it stayed until 2003 when the statue was returned to the museum in Sainshand. The value of this rare object was estimated at 24 million tugrik ($24,000). According to lore, its casting was the result of a death by stabbing at Khamaryn Khiid. After hearing the news of this death (supposedly of a Chinese man), Danzan Ravjaa created an order stating that all knives used as weapons be brought to him. The next day some 10,000 knives were piled upon his doorstep. Danzan Ravjaa then invited a silversmith from Doloon Nuur to melt the knives and with the hot metal Danzan Ravjaa's students cast the image. They brought it to life through the reading of special prayers.

The 'God of 10,000 Knives', as it is now known, is one of many artifacts on display at the Danzan Ravjaa Museum. The museum, in a former bank building, is a fascinating treasure trove of Buddhist art, textbooks, theater costumes and personal items, such as Ravjaa's pen, sword and personal seal. Most of these items came out of the unearthed boxes. Featured prominently is a painting of Ulaan Sakhios (Sanskrit: Mahakala), the Red Talisman, who served as a prominent protector deity for Danzan Ravjaa and many other Mongolian monks. One display case contains items that were destroyed during the purge: mangled deities, burnt sutras and, pointedly, a statue with what appears to be a bullet hole in its back. The center of the museum is dominated by a wax figure of Danzan Ravjaa, and in front of him sits the glass jar containing his remains. The museum is now a popular tourist attraction, but also serves as a shrine for the cult following which Danzan Ravjaa still enjoys in Dornogobi Aimag.

"When we started building the museum we thought there would be resistance by the government," Tsagaanderem explained. "People enjoyed his poetry but the government had never been open to recognizing his achievements because that would involve talking about Buddhism. But as the project continued we found the new government to be very supportive. People's minds changed in a very short time."[135]

*   *   *

Funds were also raised to build a new monastery at the site of the old Khamaryn Khiid. Altangerel wrote an article for a local newspaper and requested that the people of Dornogobi donate to the cause. The local army unit proved to be most generous, giving money, construction supplies and manpower; perhaps trying to make amends for their predecessors who destroyed the monastery some 60 years earlier.

After a month of collecting, around a hundred volunteers went to the abandoned location and built two small temples. There is a modern-day legend attached to this. It is said that in December 1990, a few months before construction was set to begin, and when nothing grows in the frozen wilderness, a beautiful lily sprouted out of the ground where Ravjaa's library had stood.

The area was declared a 'sacred zone' and hunting wild animals was prohibited. The crowning touch of the main temple was the dedication of a large statue of Padmasambhava. A small band of eight monks were employed to serve the rural temple. The head monk is Dösh, a former herder who had studied Buddhism in secret since 1960. Sh. Baatar, a Gesgui lama, is second in charge at Khamaryn Khiid. Baatar, a former worker at the Athletic Center in Sainshand, says he and the other monks have a close spiritual connection to both Buddhism and Danzan Ravjaa.

"Danzan Ravjaa's spirit is most certainly here. I wanted to join this monastery to feel his spirit," said Baatar. "I once saw Danzan Ravjaa in a dream. He was exactly as I expected him to look. He was sitting on top of a cloud and said nothing, but only blessed me with his book."

Baatar echoes the words of the other monks at Khamaryn Khiid when he says he hopes the complex will someday expand to its former glory. "There were once 500 monks here, and I believe that some day there will be 500 monks again."[136]

The most outspoken of the monks at Khamaryn Khiid is a former truck driver named B. Enkhjargal. He explains that the spirit of Danzan Ravjaa fuels his enthusiasm.

"I was drawn here by the gods and I am still waiting for my teacher to return. Our teacher is famous in Mongolia and all around the world. He has many abilities in religion, art and magic; he has the power to return water that came down from the mountains. We must learn from him and continue his work," Enkhjargal said.[137]

In 1993, a film crew spent the summer at the monastery while shooting a documentary on Danzan Ravjaa. The film had far-reaching effects in reintroducing him to Mongolia. Tsagaan was also an integral part of the resurrection of Danzan Ravjaa; she spent the twilight years of her life bridging the gap between Damdinsuren's research and what the new discoveries had to offer. She died in 1998 at the age of 75.

"The people of Dornogobi will carry on Ravjaa's memory. We

think he started our intellectual revolution. Now you can find many clever people in this province, we write well and we are talented. I think this is Ravjaa's influence," D. Bold theorized. "I think if Ravjaa were alive today our social situation would be better. Now there are many troubled people and illiterates. He could have influenced our spiritual life. Danzan Ravjaa's first plays were shown in 1827, and nearly 200 years have passed since then. I think if his work was not interrupted by Communism and the current economic problems, Mongolia would be a center of intellectualism and spirituality."[138]

*   *   *

Altangerel spent much of the 1990s producing new material about Ravjaa based on the documents hidden by his grandfather. He has been the monastery's biggest cheerleader and fundraiser. His public relations blitz has turned Khamaryn Khiid into a spiritual center that now draws a steady stream of pilgrims to the site. Altangerel was also instrumental in the renovation of the Shambhala site, which was unveiled in 2006. Shambhala, once just a simple ovoo, is now a large ring of stupas and gates circumambulated by the faithful. It is considered to be a powerful 'energy center' and pilgrims are regularly seen lying on its soil to absorb this energy. Currently Altangerel is training his teenage son Altan-Ochir (who also has an auspicious birthmark on his back) to take over his position when he reaches the age of 25.

D. Bold gives high accolades to Altangerel, "No one else in the world knows Danzan Ravjaa like Altangerel does," he says. "It is very important to listen to him and gather his stories. He is knowledgeable and clever and capable of carrying this important legacy."[139]

While Altangerel promotes various facets of Danzan Ravjaa's life, other researchers concentrate on specific areas such as Ravjaa's painting, poetry or philosophy. G. Tsagaanderem, who received a master's degree on Ravjaa's paintings, explains that the Hutagt was not bound by classic rules of Buddhist artwork. He made his own rules.

"His work was very individualistic, so it's easy to determine what was painted by his hand and what was done by his students. Ravjaa lived at the same time as some of the great European revivalists like the Russian artists A.A. Ivanov and I.Y. Repin. They were advancing art in Europe just like Ravjaa was advancing art in Mongolia, even though they never knew each other. This shows that Mongolia had its own renaissance,"[140] Tsagaanderem explains.

Some researchers, including Prof. Hurelbaatar at the Mongolian National University, consider Ravjaa's skills as a healer, painter, architect and social critic as being over-exaggerated.

"Danzan Ravjaa was a Buddhist. He was above talk about social conditions and the arts. His most publicized accomplishments were in some way used to advance his spiritual power. He realized that politics, feuding with Manchu authority and debate with other sects of Buddhism were on the path to suffering, so he swept all of that away,"[141] says Hurelbaatar.

In the book *Sutandaa Tukh Hairtai* (*History Loves Genius*), Hurelbaatar criticizes his peers for over-praising Ravjaa. He believes that Ravjaa's disciples and peers did not receive enough credit for their efforts in music and the arts. Credit for all their work, Hurelbaatar explains, was simply passed onto Ravjaa. "Danzan Ravjaa wrote song lyrics, but it was Dadishura who composed most of the music. Many of his poems were actually created by his scribes, Haliut and Jamynshagvar, who copied down Ravjaa's drunken tirades and turned them into comprehensible verse. As well, many of the paintings we attribute to Ravjaa were done by his students."[142]

The researcher suggests that the study of Ravjaa move away from what was taught during 70 years of communism. "If you want to unlock the secrets of this man you cannot use a European or Russian key, you must use an Oriental key. The most important thing is not to separate his religion and philosophy," said Hurelbaatar.

"During communism we were instructed to study Danzan Ravjaa from a historical and political point of view. We studied his song lyrics and tried to find meaning in them. But the words were just words; the real effect of the songs was the melody and energy of the singing. The sounds produced by the songs create an energy that affects the biorhythm of people and environment. For example, Danzan Ravjaa could sing songs to create rain and end drought, but it was the melody, not the words, which attracted the rain clouds," Hurelbaatar explains.

Why then did Ravjaa create a play like *Saran Khökhöö*, which showed conflicts between ranks and class relations?

"Imagine a plant. You cannot have a leaf without a stem. Therefore, you cannot explain Buddhism unless you have a method to explain it. So even though there are political elements to the story, these are only methods to explain Buddhism. Laganaa and Sersadanii were thought of as representing the cruel rule of the Manchus. It's not true. They were merely symbols of bad elements, bad karma and bad deities.

"Danzan Ravjaa can and should be studied from a philosophical and Buddhist point of view. Other methods are mere distractions."[143]

Debate about Danzan Ravjaa is heating up as more of his works are published and clearer information about his mysterious life is disseminated. Researchers were able to present some of their findings at a conference to honor the 200-year anniversary of Ravjaa's birth, held in 2003. The event was a celebration of sorts: a tribute to a man who in the face of persecution defended his nation, a man who respected women and the poor, and a renaissance man who developed Mongolian arts and culture. Two hundred years after his birth, Mongolia's democratic revolution provided researchers the opportunity to study these aspects of his life and clutch the missing links of his history.

The following poem, written by the late writer and politician O. Dashbalbar, provides a lyrical view of Ravjaa for the modern era.

> He was a man of the world
> Not just one river but all the oceans
> Not just one piece of land but mountains, continents,
> Islands and steppes belong to him
>
> He loved not just one group of people
> But all animals under heaven
> His love did not know the limit of the eight directions
> The galaxies of wandering stars weren't enough for his love
>
> He lived at the same time as Pushkin
> Each of them had their own body
> The distance between them was great
> But they breathed the same air and had the same desire:
> freedom

He didn't meet Pushkin and never heard his name
Pushkin also did not meet the great poet Ravjaa
Although in different parts of the world
They saw the sun and moon with the same eyes

Animals and the Gobi Desert were close to him
Love and books were close to him
He loved people and freedom
The Gobi Lord came through these doors
The river of beautiful women and
Images of the gods were his friends
He could escape the badness of the world
Leave the wheel of life and be free

Now he lives in the peace of eternity, and
Closed the door to the lower world
When he was alive he didn't support bad leadership
Ravjaa is the power to escape living

He understood that the world deceives
So he made vodka, women and intellectuals his friends
His consciousness was against violence,
And he even challenged the Bogd Gegeen

Because of freedom he could even oppose his Buddha
Ravjaa was eager to become Buddha
He preferred physical and spiritual freedom
Great lyricist Ravjaa.

Epilogue

An important question regarding Danzan Ravjaa's legacy persists today. What became of all those boxes buried by Lama Tuduv and the other monks of Khamaryn Khiid? At least three boxes (perhaps as many as five) were found and destroyed in 1969. Altangerel uncovered 32 boxes in 1990. This means that at least 15 chests remain buried in the earth, preserved and protected by the Gobi.

Only Altangerel knows the precise number of boxes, their contents and location. He remains cagey with this sensitive information to ensure the security of the boxes. Altangerel insists that the boxes will remain in the desert until the museum is properly financed and equipped to deal with such an important undertaking. Without adequate funding, the museum cannot afford secure display cases or a high-quality alarm system.

The Mongolian government offers little support for the operation of the museum and Altangerel has relied on private donations to maintain the facilities. From the early 2000s, sufficient funds were raised to build a new museum in Sainshand, which opened in 2008. Despite the expanded and improved facilities, Altangerel is not entirely convinced of its security and has chosen to keep some of the boxes in the desert.

Altangerel still dreams of rebuilding the White Temple at Khamaryn Khiid to house the remainder of the collection. He came one step closer to achieving this dream in 2009 when a donation came his way, thanks to a unique media event. On August 1, 2009, a group of Austrian Buddhist adventurers trekked down to Khamaryn Khiid and recorded the excavation of two of the remaining crates. The event was covered live on the Internet through a satellite transmission feed from the Gobi. The undertaking can be seen again on www.gobi-treasure.com.

The Gobi Treasure Hunt, as it was dubbed, was not quite like discovering unknown lost riches; Altangerel had known the location and contents of the boxes for years. Nevertheless, it was an exciting media event that did much to raise awareness of Danzan Ravjaa's legacy outside of Mongolia. All donations collected during the event were delivered to the Danzan Ravjaa Museum.

This story remains unfinished. More boxes remain in the desert, hiding their secrets for another day.

"When the time is right," says Altangerel, these crates will be drawn from the earth, properly researched and displayed again for the benefit of the Gobi people.

The original Danzan Ravjaa Museum in Sainshand

Chronology

1734   Saran Khökhöö Namtar is written in Tibet.

1750s   Qing Dynasty gains control over whole Mongol territory.

1793   New Manchu law allows hutagts to be born in common families.

1800   Fourth Noyon Hutagt executed.

1803   Ravjaa is born into a common family.

1809   Ravjaa is recognized as the rebirth of the Fourth Noyon Hutagt but, to safeguard his life, is also given the title of Avshaa Gegeen.

1812   Ravjaa meets the Bogd Gegeen, who names him 'Luvson Danzan Ravjaa'.

1817   Danzan Ravjaa studies in Alasha.

1820   Fifth Bogd Gegeen enthroned.

1820   Danzan Ravjaa commissions Khamaryn Khiid.

1821   Ravjaa's only surviving parent dies.

1822   Ravjaa commissions the Labrang süm in the Ordos region.

1825   Ravjaa visits Doloon Nuur with 100 disciples.

1825   Danzan Ravjaa writes the 'The Kite.'

1826   Danzan Ravjaa lives in Peking.

1827-28 Danzan Ravjaa adapts the libretto Saran Khökhöö Namtar for a Mongolian audience.

1828   Danzan Ravjaa travels to Doloon Nuur and Chahar region of China. Later this year he starts the construction of Gurvan Galbiin Khiid.

1829   Danzan Ravjaa visits Chahar to study tsam and painting.

1830   Danzan Ravjaa visits his temples in Outer Mongolia.

1831   Danzan Ravjaa studies theater in Alasha, makes his first visit to Agui Süm and goes on pilgrimage to Kumbun Monastery in Amdo.

1832   Danzan Ravjaa briefly visits Huree.

1833   Danzan Ravjaa returns to Agui Süm to excavate and renovate the site.

1834   Danzan Ravjaa winters in Peking. Construction of the Khamaryn Khiid theater is complete.

1836   Danzan Ravjaa travels in southern Gobi Mergen Van and Chahar.

1839   Danzan Ravjaa cures the Fifth Bogd Gegeen of an ailment.

1841   Fifth Bogd Gegeen holds an audience with the Manchu Emperor.

1841   Danzan Ravjaa attempts to reach Lhasa, but is called back by the Janjiya Hutagt of Doloon Nuur.

1842   Danzan Ravjaa builds the Givaadinravjaaling Treasury (the White Temple).

1842-1844 French missionary Abbé Huc travels in Manchu China.

1843   Danzan Ravjaa visits Gurvan Galbiin Khiid.

1846   Danzan Ravjaa visits the hot spring area near modern-day Arvaikheer. In this same year he also visits Doloon Nuur and Gurvan Galbiin Khiid.

1850   Danzan Ravjaa visits Gurvan Galbiin Khiid and Alasha.

1852   Danzan Ravjaa performs a religious ceremony to help end the Taiping Rebellion.

1853   Danzan Ravjaa gathers his disciples at 'Shambhala' and predicts his death.

1854   Danzan Ravjaa commissions the Ordu Huree in Ulaanshand. He later travels to Ongiin Gol and then Huree.

1855   Sixth Noyon Hutagt born.

1856   Danzan Ravjaa dies.

1873   Eighth Bogd Gegeen enthroned.

1875   Sixth Noyon Hutagt dies.

1891   Seventh Noyon Hutagt is born.

1911   Qing Dynasty falls and Mongolia gains nominal independence.

1931   Seventh Noyon Hutagt is arrested for 'counter-revolutionary' activities.

1938   Khamaryn Khiid is destroyed by the order of Mongolia's Communist government.

1950s   History professor Damdinsuren revives Danzan Ravjaa studies.

1990   Curator Tuduv dies.

1991   Khamaryn Khiid is re-opened with one temple.

2003   Celebrations held for the 200th anniversary of Danzan Ravjaa's birth.

2005   Shambhala is reconstructed.

GOBI NOYON HUTAGTS and LIFE DATES

1. Agvangonchig   (1621-1703)
2. Jamyn Dambi Jantzen   (1704-1739)
3. Jamyn Danzan   (1740-1765)
4. Jamyn Oidov Jampts   (1765-1800)
5. Luvson Danzan Ravjaa   (1803-1856)
6. Luvson Dambi Jantzen Odser   (1855-1875)
7. Agvan Luvsan Dambi Jantzen   (1891-1931)
8. Samdan Jampts   (1933-1945)

NOYON HUTAGT PRE-INCARNATIONS

1. Bodan Choglai Namjil
2. Genendarma
3. Zanjod Hiruga
4. Lodoidambsamburavdan
5. Jamchivsembaajila Jeradorj
6. Zanaadaraa
7. Lovongaravdorje
8. Shivarii
9. Duvchingugurii (Guru Kukuripa)
10. Lovon Shagjaashiinen
11. Agiivanchug
12. Seseribaa
13. Duvtov Deshri
14. Lochen Vero Zana
15. Ganing Shidag Dorje Balden
16. Serjiizunbaa
17. Duvchin Namhaidorj
18. Tudevajir
19. Duvtov Darchinchar
20. Lamaashan
21. Danagdorj
22. Karmapa Rolpe Dorje
23. Ronsomchoi
24. Nyamral
25. Lodoisingii
26. Tsarchin
27. Zanindraa
28. Siriiravjii

29. Gungadorje
30. Sanjaibalsan

DANZAN RAVJAA TAKHILCH (Curators) and LIFE DATES
1. Balchinchoijoo 1804 – 1865 (61 years)
2. Gan-Ochir 1837 – 1889 (52 years)
3. Naria 1861 – 1900 (39 years)
4. Ongoi 1890 – 1931 (41 years)
5. Tuduv 1912 – 1990 (78 years)
6. Altangerel b.1960 –

THE PRINCES OF GOBI MERGEN VAN HOSHUU

Name	Years in power	Year started rule
Gursikheh	13	1692
Ravdandorj	23	1705
Minjuurdorj	12	1728
Tserenbaituv	15	1740
Danzadorj	17	1755
Chavagadorj	7	1772
Dorjjav	38	1779
Dagdandorj	9	1818
Lasurenbazar	48	1827
Amgaabazar	17	1875
Anandochir	20	1892
Tsesunjav	6	1912
Bat-Ochir	5	1923

BOGD GEGEENS OF URGA and LIFE DATES
1. Zanabazar (1653-1723)
2. Losang Tenbey Dronmey (1724-1757)
3. Yeshe Tenbey Nyima (1758-1773)
4. Losang Tupten Wongchuk (1775-1813)
5. Losang Tsultrim Jikmey (1815-1842)
6. Losang Palden Tenpa (1842-1849)
7. Ngawang Chokyi Wongchuk Trinley Gyatsho (1850-1868)
8. Ngawang Losang Chokyi Nyima Tenzin Wongchuk (1870-1924)

DALAI LAMAS and LIFE DATES
1. Gendundrup (1391-1475)

2. Gedun Gyatsho   (1475-1542)
3. Sonam Gyatsho   (1543-1588)
4. Yonten Gyatsho   (1589-1617)
5. Ngawang Losang Gyatsho (1617-1682)
6. Tsangyang Gyatsho   (1683-1746, deposed 1706)
7. Kelzang Gyatsho   (1708-1757)
8. Jampel Gyatsho   (1758-1804)
9. Lungton Gyatsho   (1806-1815)
10. Tsultrim Gyatsho   (1816-1837)
11. Khendrup Gyatsho   (1838-1856)
12. Trinley Gyatsho   (1856-1875)
13. Thubten Gyatsho   (1876-1933)
14. Tenzing Gyatsho   (born 1935)

PANCHEN LAMAS and LIFE DATES
Khendrub Je   (1385-1438)
Sonam Choklang   (1438-1505)
Losang Dondrup   (1505-1568)
Losang Chokyi   (1569-1662)
Losang Yeshe   (1663-1737)
Losang Palden Yeshe   (1737-1780)
Tenpai Nyima   (1781-1852)
Palden Chokyi Drakpa   (1853-1882)
Gelek Namgyal   (1883-1937)
Losang Chokyi Gyaltsen   (1938-1989)
Gedhun Coekyi Nyima   (born 1995)

QING EMPERORS and REIGN DATES
Shunzhi   (1644-61)
Kangxi   (1662-1722)
Yongzheng   (1723-35)
Qianlong   (1736-95)
Jiaqing   (1796-1820)
Daoguang   (1821-50)
Xianfong   (1851-61)
Tungzhi   (1862-74)
Kuangxu   (1875-1908)
Xuantung   (1909-11)

GLOSSARY

Ace-lhamo – Buddhist morality play.

Abbé Huc – French missionary who traveled in Inner Mongolia, 1842-1844.

Agvangonchig – the first Noyon Hutagt.

Albutu – common person, nomad.

Airag – fermented mare's milk.

Alasha – An area of western Inner Mongolia, frequently visited by Danzan Ravjaa.

Amgalan Monastery – temple complex commissioned by the first Noyon Hutagt.

Arats – impoverished herders and peasants.

Badarchin – wanderer.

Blue Faith – Cult created by Van Tuden, an early 20th century Mongol aristocrat. Elements of hedonism and the drinking of blood were involved.

Bogd Gegeen – the head of the Gelugpa sect in Mongolia.

Bön – animist religion in Tibet before Buddhism.

Buduun – Fat, overweight.

Choilong Monastery – temple complex in Dornogobi Aimag, commissioned by the second Noyon Hutagt.

Dogshin – literally: terrible. When making reference to Danzan Ravjaa it can mean "fierce," or, as some scholars allege, "genius."

Doloon Nuur – city in Inner Mongolia, home to the Janjiya Hutagt.

Dornogobi – a province in southeast Mongolia where Khamaryn Khiid is located.

Ger – felt tent used by nomads.

Gelugpa – reformed sect of Tibetan Buddhism founded by Tsongkhapa in the 14th century. The Dalai Lama leads this sect, which is also known as 'yellow hat.'

Gurvan Galbiin Khiid – monastery complex built by Danzan Ravjaa in south Gobi.

Huree – old name of Mongolia's capital Ulaanbaatar.

Huvilgan – incarnation of a senior lama.

Jamyn Danzan – third Noyon Hutagt, executed at the age of 25.

Janjiya Hutagt – Head Lama of Doloon Nuur.

Kargyupa – sect of Tibetan Buddhism, also known as 'red hats.' This sect is more contemplative than the more scholarly Gelugpa.

Khalkh – the largest Mongol ethnic group, and the area of modern-day central Mongolia.

Khamaryn Khiid – monastery built by Danzan Ravjaa in 1821.

Khashant Khiid – Gobi monastery that was home to the fourth Noyon Hutagt.

Khiid – monastery.

Lang – a weight measurement equaling 37.2 grams.

Li-Fan-Yuan – Chinese Ministry of Mongolian and Tibetan Affairs.

Manchus – nomadic tribesmen from areas lying east of Mongolia and north of Peking. Founders of China's Qing Dynasty.

Naadam – sports festival (archery, horse racing, wrestling).

Noyon Hutagt – Lord Saint.

Ongiin Gol Khiid – monastery that hosted Danzan Ravjaa's ordination in 1809. Located in Dundgobi Aimag.

Qing – a Manchurian Dynasty that ruled China and Mongolia. The Qing ruled from 1644-1911.

Saran Khökhöö – Moon Cuckoo.

Shav – serfs owned by huvilgans.

Shulmuss – female devil.

Stupa – a white monument with a square base and a top with overlying cylindrical shapes, representing the universe.

Surgaal – precept, instructions from a teacher to his students.

Süm – temple.

Tantra – a method of Buddhist meditation which allows the possibility of immediate realization.

Tsam – a religious dance performed by monks.

Yansang Yidam – the Buddhist deity associated with the Gobi Noyon Hutagt incarnates.

Administration

Aimag = Province.

Khoshuu = Banner (county).

Sum = Military division of 150 men. The number of sum in a khoshuu was between one and ten.

Otog = Unit where shav live.

Names of Aristocratic Classes

Khaan – ruled one of the seven Khalkh khoshuu.

Chin Van – held 60 bondmen.

Jung Van – held 50 bondmen.

Beil – held 40 bondmen.

Beis – held 35 bondmen.

Gun – held 30 bondmen.

Zasag-taij – eldest son of a nobleman.

Names of Buddhist Classes

Gegeen – huvilgan who has displayed extraordinary efforts of civil merit.

Lama – a non-ordained monk.

Hutagt – a reincarnated saint with special recognition from the Manchu court in Peking.

Tamagtai hutagt – a hutagt with a special seal indicating that he owns a certain amount of land including shav.

Tamagui hutagt – a hutagt without a seal and small numbers of shav. They are subordinate to the local administration. Usually known simply as huvilgan.

Bibliography

Books

Andrews, R.C. *Across Mongolian Plains: A Naturalist's Account of China's "Great Northwest."* New York. D. Appleton and Company, 1921.

Baatar, D. *Tavdugaar Dogshin Noyon Hutagt Rabjiin Tsedeg.* Ulaanbaatar, Shudar Printing House, 1993.

Bawden, C.R. *The Modern History of Mongolia,* New York. Fredrick A. Praeger Publishers, 1968.

Damdinsuren, Ts. *Mongoliin Uran Zokhioliin Ov Ulamjaliin Asuudalud* (p. 68-107). Edited by Kh. Sampildendev. Published by Shinjilekh Ukhanii Akademii Khevlel. Ulaanbaatar 1984.

Danzan Ravjaa. *Gobiin Dogshin Noyon Hutagtiin Aildsan Manlai Moriin Erdeniin Shinj Khemeekh Sudaar Orshvai.* ed. Z. Altangerel. Ulaanbaatar. Sudar Printing House, 1998.

Danzan Ravjaa. *Saran Khökhöö*, p. 404-424. *Paper Bird* p. 446. Life biography p. 445. Ulaanbaatar. Zuun Bileg, 1944.

Danzan Ravjaa. *Ulemchiin Chanar.* Compiled by Ts. Bandihuu, edited by D. Baatar. Yaralt Sonin Printing Press. Sainshand. 1991.

Danzan Ravjaa. Yaruu Nairgiin Zurkh. ed. Sh. Gaadamba. Ulaanbaatar. Suudriin Chuulagan Printing House. 1993.

Danzan Ravjaa. *Yaruu Nairgiin Tsomorlog.* Collected by D. Tsagaan, edited by D. Yondon. Ulaanbaatar. Soyombo Printing House, 1992.

Danzan Ravjaa., *Zokhioliin Emkhtgel.* ed. Ts. Damdinsuren and D. Tsagaan. Ulaanbaatar. State Committee on Publishing Affairs, 1962.

Dowman, Keith. *Masters of Mahamudra*. Albany. State University of New York Press, 1985.

Gilmour, James. *Among the Mongols*. New York. London Tract Society, 1883.

Hedin, Sven. *My Life as an Explorer*. New York. Kodansha America Inc, 1996.

Heissig, Walther. *A Lost Civilization: the Mongols Rediscovered*. (p. 211-230) London. Thames and Hudson, 1966.

Howarth, Sir Henry. *History of the Mongols: From the 9th to 19th Century Part IV*. Burt Franklin, New York, 1927.

Huc, Abbé. *Travels in Tartary, Thibet and China 1844-1846*. George Routledge & Sons, Ltd. Broadway House, Carter Lane, London, vol. one and two, 1928.

Hutagtiin Tukhai Khuuch. ed. Altangerel and Tsagaanderem. Ulaanbaatar. Printed by Ulsiin Standartiin Khevlekh Uildver, 1995.

Jones, M. *Life and Travels in Tartary, Thibet and China* (Being a Narrative of the Abbe Huc's travels in the Far East). T. Nelson and Sons, London, 1872.

Lemunyon, Edmund. Original book source unknown. *The Lama and the Motor car*.

Lhavgasuren, G. *Noyon Hutagt Danzan Ravjaa*. Ulaanbaatar. Government Publishing House, 1993.

Manchen-Helfen, Otto. *Journey to Tuva*. University of California, Ethnographic Press, 1992.

Mongol Nutag Dakh Tuukh Soel Dursgal... (Korean/Mongolian textbook)

Petitions of Grievances Submitted by the People. Translated by S. Rasidondug in collaboration with Veronika Veit. Otto Harrassowitz-Wiesbadan, 1975.

Pozdneyev, A.M. *Mongolia and the Mongols*, Indiana University, Bloomington, 1971.

Przewalski, N. Mongolia, *The Tangut Country, and the Solitudes of Northern Tibet*, Translated by E. Delmar Morgan, vol. 1. London: Sampson Low, Marston, Searle & Rivington, 1876.

Roerich, George N. *Trails to Inmost Asia*. New Haven. Yale University Press, 1931.

Sutandaa Tuukh Khairtai. Collected works. Ulaanbaatar. Mongolian Knowledge University Press, 1998.

Tsagaan, D. *D. Rabjagiin Tgaruu Nairgiin Zokhioliin Toim*, Ulaanbaatar. Press of Academy of Sciences, 1955.

Reports

Bawden C.R. "Notes on the Ranks and Titles of the Mongol Nobility During Manchu Times," Naples, 1970.

Bawden C.R. "Remarks on some Contemporary Performances of Epics in the MPR," London, 1969.

Bawden C.R. "Some Documents Concerning the Complement of Manchu Companies at Chapu in the mid-19th century." Otto Harrossowitz, No. 18, 1985.

Charleux, Isabelle. "Mongol Pilmages to Wutaishan in the late Qing Dynasty." Journal of International Tibetan Studies, 2009.

Charleux, Isabelle. "Padmasambhava's Travel to the North," p. 168-232. Central Asiatic Journal. No 46, 2 (2002).

Heissig, Walther. "History of Mongolian Literature." Weisbaden, Otto Harrassowitz. 1966.

Kiripolska, Marta. "Icige, icige (A Poem of Danjin Rabjai)." 2001.

Kiripolska, Marta. "Who was Dulduitu (A Note on Rabjai)." 1999.

Morrow, Peter. "Preserving the Legacy of Danzan Ravjaa, Lord of the Gobi." Tibet Foundation Newsletter. 2002.

Pozdneyev, Aleksei M. "Religion and Ritual in Society: Lamaist Buddhism in Late 19th Century Mongolia." Publications of the Mongolia Society, Inc. Edited by John R. Krueger. Occasional Papers, No. 10. Bloomington, Indiana, 1978.

Rupen, Robert. "The City of Urga in the Manchu Period," Weisbaden, Otto Harrassowitz, 1957.

Serruys, Henry. "A Document from 1904 Dismissing an Ordos Prince from Office." *Central Asiatic Journal,* Vol. XIX No. 3, 1975. Otto

Harrassowitz, p. 206.

Strong, Anna Louise. "Old and New Gods in Mongolia." *Asia Journal*, vol. 28 p. 564.

Tsagaan, D. "On Humanism in Some Works Known as Surgaals." (Essay found at Danzan Ravjaa Museum, publisher and date unknown)

Underdown, Michael. "Banditry and Revolutionary Movements in Late 19th and Early 20th Century Mongolia." Mongolian Studies, Indiana University, vol. VI p. 109-116. 1980.

Newspapers

The Mongol Messenger. Nov. 3, 1999 (No. 44, 434).

The Mongol Messenger. Oct. 18, 2000. (No. 42, 484).

Yaralt, August 1993 (No. 28, 3720).

Yaralt, February 1998 (No. 5, 3858).

Internet

Encyclopaedia Britannica (www.britannica.com), Buddhism, Central Asian Arts.

Don Croner: www.doncroner.com.

ENDNOTES

1   Huc, p. 48.

2   This verse is from a poem called "A Mirror of Wisdom," found on p. 240 of 'An Anthology of Danzan Ravjaa's Poetry,' compiled (in Mongolian) by D. Tsagaan and published in Mongolia in 1992 with the title 'A Mirror of Wisdom'. The translation, unpublished is by Batbold Baast.

3   Danzan Ravjaa, *Yaruu Nairgiin Tsomorlog* p. 52.

4   Some scholars contend that when referring to certain personalities such as Ravjaa, Dogshin is better defined as "Genius."

5   Pozdneyev, p. 333.

6   There is one photograph of a teenage boy that is said to be Ravjaa, and is often included in books about him. However, the picture is almost certainly not Ravjaa as his teenage years were several decades before the first cameras arrived in Mongolia.

7   Modern-day Hövsgöl sum, Dornogobi Aimag.

8   *Van* is a term that means lord. In this sentence, the Gobi Mergen Van is the head of Gobi Mergen Van khoshuu.

9   Another version says a lama named Tserenbaazar ignited the fire.

10 Pozdneyev, p. 361.

11 *Ulemchin Chanar* newspaper p. 13

12 Danzan Ravjaa, *Yaruu Nairgiin Tsomorlog*, p. 91. Note that this poem is also found in Danzan Ravjaa's collected works, which calls into question its true author. While Gobi legend attributes the piece to Jamyn Oidov Jampts, scholars would argue that the poem belonged to Ravjaa.

13 Roerich, *Trails to Inmost Asia*, p. 185.

14 Some historians have written that Ravjaa's mother died in childhood. A new school of thought suggests that she raised him by herself, a matter discussed in chapter 3.

15 *Hutagtiin Tukhai Khuuch*, p. 11.

16   Danzan Ravjaa, *Yaruu Nairgiin Tsomorlog*, p. 85.

17   Heissig, *History of Mongolian Literature* p. 189.

18   Pozdneyev, *Religion and Ritual in Society*, p. 344.

19   Kiripolska "Who was Dulduitu" p. 102-3.

20   Heissig, *History of Mongolian Literature*. p. 190.

21   *Khutagiin Tukhai Huuch,* p. 13.

22   Damdinsuren, *Mongoliin Uran… Asuudalud.* p. 81.

23   Baatar, p. 35.

24   Huc, p. 32.

25   Croner, webpage, "China / Inner Mongolia / Doloon Nuur".

26   Pozdneyev, "Mongolia and the Mongols," vol. 2 p. 193.

27   Taken from local literature on Doloon Nuur city.

28   Charleux, Isabelle. "Mongol Pilgrimages to Wutaishan in the late Qing Dynasty".

29   Pozdneyev, p. 350.

30   Descriptions of the Cave Temple are sourced from the report "Padmasambhava's Travel to the North", written by Isabelle Charleux, published by Central Asiatic Journal 46, 2 (2002) p. 168-232.

31   *Mongol Nutag Dakh Tukh Soel Dursgal* p. 266-7.

32   Danzan Ravjaa, *Zokioliin Emekhtgel* p. 120.

33   Interview, June 2001.

34   *Sutandaa Tukh Hairtai*, p. 61.

35   *Sutandaa Tukh Hairtai*, p. 65.

36   *Sutandaa Tukh Hairtai*, p. 27.

37   Huc, p. 33-34.

38   Danzan Ravjaa, *Yaruu Nairgiin Tsomorlog*, p. 173.

39   Howarth, p. 72.

40   Howarth, p. 73.

41   Lhavgasuren, p. 16.

42   Huc, p. 139-140.

43   The translation of this poem varies as more than one version of the poem has been found in the original Mongol. Also note that the work itself is not completely original. Some verses were originally composed by the Third Mergen Gegeen (1717-1766).

44   Bawden, *The Modern History of Mongolia*, p. 386.

45   Przewalski, p. 69.

46   Bawden, "Remarks on Some Contemporary Performances," p. 39.

47   Gilmour, p. 268-269.

48   Krueger, p. 80.

49 Damdinsuren, *Mongoliin Uran Zokhioliin Ov Ulamjaliin Asuudalud*, p. 94-95. In this play, Palgye Dorje was actually named Lhaladbaldorj.

50 Interview, June 2001.

51 Danzan Ravjaa, *Yaruu Nairgiin Tsomorlog*, p. 264.

52 Heissig, *A Lost Civilization: The Mongols Rediscovered* p. 218.

53 Damdinsuren, *Mongoliin Uran Zokhioliin Ov Ulamjaliin Asuudalud*, p. 96.

54 Dogmid, *The Mongol Messenger*.

55 Damdinsuren, *Mongoliin Uran Zokhioliin Ov Ulamjaliin Asuudalud*, p. 94-95.

56 Heissig, *A Lost Civilization, The Mongols Rediscovered* p. 214.

57 Heissig, *History of Mongolian Literature*, Vol 1, p. 216.

58 Named Sain Altan in the 1770 translation.

59 Named Ekshig in the 1770 translation.

60 *Sutandaa Tukh Hairtai*, p. 24.

61 In the 1770 version, the cuckoo does not die but remains faithful to the birds by staying among them to preach Buddhism.

62 *Sutandaa Tukh Hairtai*, p. 22.

63 *Sutandaa Tukh Hairtai*, pp. 24-25.

64 *Zokioliin Emekhtgel*, p. 339.

65 Damdinsuren, *Mongoliin Uran Zokhioliin Ov Ulamjaliin Asuudalud*, p. 95.

66 *Yaralt* newspaper, 1993.

67 *Yaralt*, 1993, p. 3.

68 Danzan Ravjaa, *Yaruu Nairgiin Tsomorlog* p. 100.

69 *History of Mongolian Literature*, p. 203.

70 *Sutandaa Tukh Hairtai*, p. 59.

71 Meaning, her perfect body, owned by the writer.

72 Danzan Ravjaa, *Yaruu Nairgiin Tsomorlog*, p. 41.

73 Lhavgasuren, p. 95.

74 Danzan Ravjaa, *Yaruu Nairgiin Tsomorlog* p. 100.

75 "Humanism in Some Works Known as Surgaals" (a report).

76 Danzan Ravjaa, *Zokioliin Emkhtgel* p. 279.

77 Bawden, p. 170.

78 Bawden, p. 171.

79 *Sutandaa Tukh Hairtai*, p. 67-68.

80 Danzan Ravjaa, *Yaruu Nairgiin Tsomorlog*, p. 43.

81 Ones with fine voices are probably birds.

82 Danzan Ravjaa, *Yaruu Nairgiin Tsomorlog* p. 262.

83 Danzan Ravjaa, *Yaruu Nairgiin Tsomorlog* p. 92.

84 Baatar, *Yaralt* newspaper, 1998.

85 Danzan Ravjaa, *Yaruu Nairgiin Tsomorlog,* p. 105.

86 *Hutagtiin Tukhai Khuuch*, p. 25.

87 Interview, September 2000.

88 Interview, February 2000.

89 *Hutagtiin Tukhai Khuuch*, pp. 36-37.

90 Interview with Lovon Lam Dösh, February 2000.

91 Interview with Baast Batbold, May 2003.

92 Interview with Baast Batbold, May 2003.

93 Danzan Ravjaa, *Yaruu Nairgiin Tsomorlog,* p. 60.

94 *Sutandaa Tukh Hairtai,* p. 49.

95 *Sutandaa Tukh Hairtai,* p. 45.

96 *Sutandaa Tukh Hairtai,* p. 68.

97 Chi-Tien lived in Hangzhou at the time of the Southern Song Dynasty (1127-1279). He was considered an incarnate Bodhisattva who flouted Buddhist doctrine by eating meat and leading an unrestrained life, but was known for aiding the poor and downtrodden. He is best known as the hero of Jigong Zhuan (Biography of Master Jidian), written during the late Qing Dynasty.

98 Heissig, *History of Mongolian Literature,* vol. 1. p. 186.

99 Interview with D. Bold, June 2001.

100 Interview with D. Bold, June 2001.

101 Interview with Baast Batbold, May 2003.

102 Heissig, *History of Mongolian Literature,* vol. 1. p. 220.

103 Huc, p. 372.

104 *Hutagtiin Tukhai Khuuch*, p. 28-29.

105 Interview with D. Bold, June 2001.

106 *Hutagtiin Tukhai Khuuch*, p. 33.

107 *Hutagtiin Tukhai Khuuch*, p. 26-27.

108 Interview with Lovon Lam Dösh, February 2000.

109 Interview with D. Bold, June 2001.

110 Danzan Ravjaa, *Yaruu Nairgiin Tsomorlog* p. 100.

111 Danzan Ravjaa, *Yaruu Nairgiin Tsomorlog* p. 49.

112 Underdown, pp. 111.

113 Information from *Hutagtiin Tukhai Huuch,* p. 14-15, and interview with Altangerel, February 2000.

114 Information from *Hutagtiin Tukhai Huuch,* p. 40, and interview with Altangerel, June 2001.

115 About eight kilometers west of Zuunbayan.

116 *Hutagtiin Tukhai Khuuch*, p. 23-24.

117 Gilmour, p. 140.

118 Heissig, *History of Mongolian Literature*. p. 198-99.

119 Danzan Ravjaa, *Yaruu Nairgiin Tsomorlog*. p. 46.

120 The date, 1853, might be a mistake; 40 years would be 1861, five years after his death.

121 Danzan Ravjaa, *Yaruu Nairgiin Tsomorlog*. p. 202.

122 Heissig, *History of Literature*, vol. 1 p. 210.

123 Tsagaan, *Ravjaagiin Tgaruu Nairgiin Zokhioliin Toim*, introduction.

124 Danzan Ravjaa, *Yaruu Nairgiin Tsomorlog*, p. 171.

125 *Khutagiin Tukhai Khuuch*, p. 46.

126 Document from Danzan Ravjaa Museum, Sainshand.

127 Interview with Altangerel, June 2001.

128 *Ulemchin Chanar newspaper,* May 2003.

129 Interview, June 2001.

130 Interview, March 2000.

131 *Yaralt*, 1998.

132 Interview, June 2001.

133 Some descriptions of Tuduv and Altangerel from Peter Morrow's article "Preserving the Legacy of Danzan Ravjaa, Lord of the Gobi."

134 Interview, June 2001.

135 Interview, June 2001.

136 Interview, June 2001.

137 Interview, June 2001.

138 Interview, June 2001.

139 Interview, June 2001.

140 Interview, June 2001.

141 Interview, October 2000.

142 *Sutandaa Tukh Hairtai,* p. 77.

143 Interview, October 2000.

ACKNOWLEDGEMENTS

Several people have helped me to create this book, most notably the trustee of the Danzan Ravjaa Museum in Sainshand, Z. Altangerel, his co-worker D. Bold, and all the lamas of Khamaryn Khiid. Great thanks are also owed to translators B. Batbayar and Ts. Munkhhuyag at the Montsame News Agency in Ulaanbaatar. Ts. Tsendsuren (Tsegi) from the University of the Humanities put in a tremendous amount of work translating legends, stories and interviews. I applaud her enthusiasm for the subject. My wife Baigalmaa worked tirelessly to see the project through to the end, kept up all my contacts when I was away, and made a trip with me to Sainshand. This book would have been impossible if not for the hard work of these people.

Baljiryn Dogmid wrote the story in the *Mongol Messenger* that introduced me to Danzan Ravjaa. The staff of the *Mongol Messenger* and the Montsame News Agency supported my earlier research while Brigitte Cummings helped with material written in German. Thanks to those who made comments on the early drafts: Chris Kaplonski, Thubten Gyatso and Jane Kos. Magda Szpindler and Baast Batbold, both in Ulaanbaatar, assisted during the later drafts and helped with poetry translation. Tunga at the Central Library in Ulaanbaatar gave me access to important books and texts. Simon Wikham-Smith edited the final draft.

Thanks to Pete Spurrier and Blacksmith Books for bringing this book to light, and Glenn Mullin for seeing the project through. Thanks to friends and family in California, to my parents for their support in this endeavor. Most of all, thanks to Danzan Ravjaa, an enigmatic character whose spirit, I am sure, is still alive.

Michael Kohn was born and raised in California. He earned a BA in Literature from UC Santa Barbara in 1995. After teaching English in Japan and extensive travels in Southeast Asia, he moved to Mongolia where he worked for three years (1998–2000) as an editor for the *Mongol Messenger* newspaper. He continues to spend a part of each year in Mongolia,  reporting for media organizations such as AFP, BBC Radio, the *South China Morning Post* and the *San Francisco Chronicle*.

Michael is author of the *Lonely Planet Guide to Mongolia* as well as *Dateline Mongolia: An American Journalist In Nomad's Land*. He lives in San Francisco with his wife and daughter, and has a website at www.michaelkohn.us.